CARRY ON AMBULANCE

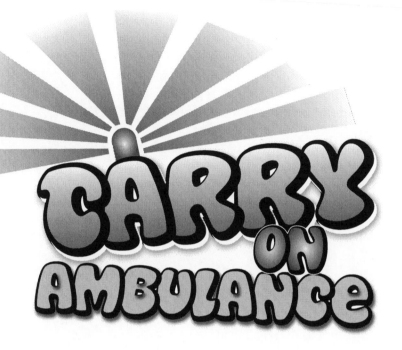

MEMOIRS
Cirencester

Published by Memoirs

MEMOIRS
PUBLISHING

Memoirs Books

25 Market Place, Cirencester, Gloucestershire, GL7 2NX
info@memoirsbooks.co.uk www.memoirspublishing.com

Copyright ©Allan Dawson, April 2012
First published in England, April 2012
Book jacket design Ray Lipscombe

ISBN: 978-1-908223-94-4

Printed in England

CARRY ON AMBULANCE

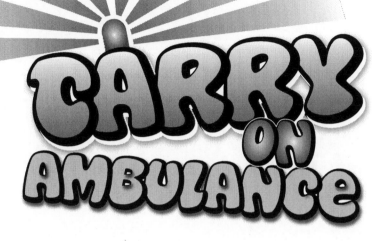

CONTENTS

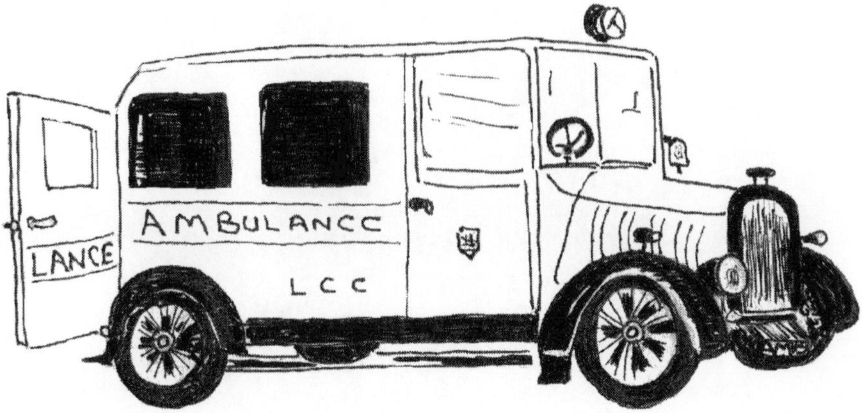
LANCE
AMBULANCC
LCC

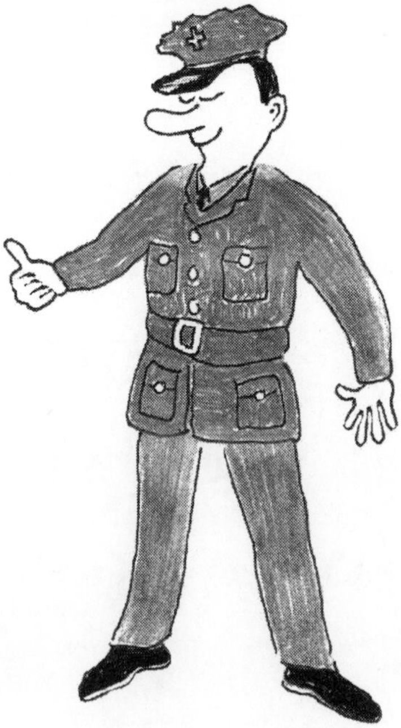

THE 1960'S

A 'CURRENT' PROBLEM

An ambulance crew were attending an obviously-deceased patient who had drowned. The crew was due off duty in 20 minutes, and the transporting of the body as well as the endless paperwork would have meant a minimum of a two-hour late finish.

The county boundary was clearly defined as a bridge crossing the river. The body had been floating with the current, but had caught on a branch ten feet upstream of the boundary. One of the ambulance men attempted to unhook the deceased patient's tangled jacket, but, in doing so he 'accidentally' released the body to float into the next county.

The neighbouring ambulance authority had to deal with the deceased. And the crew finished on time.

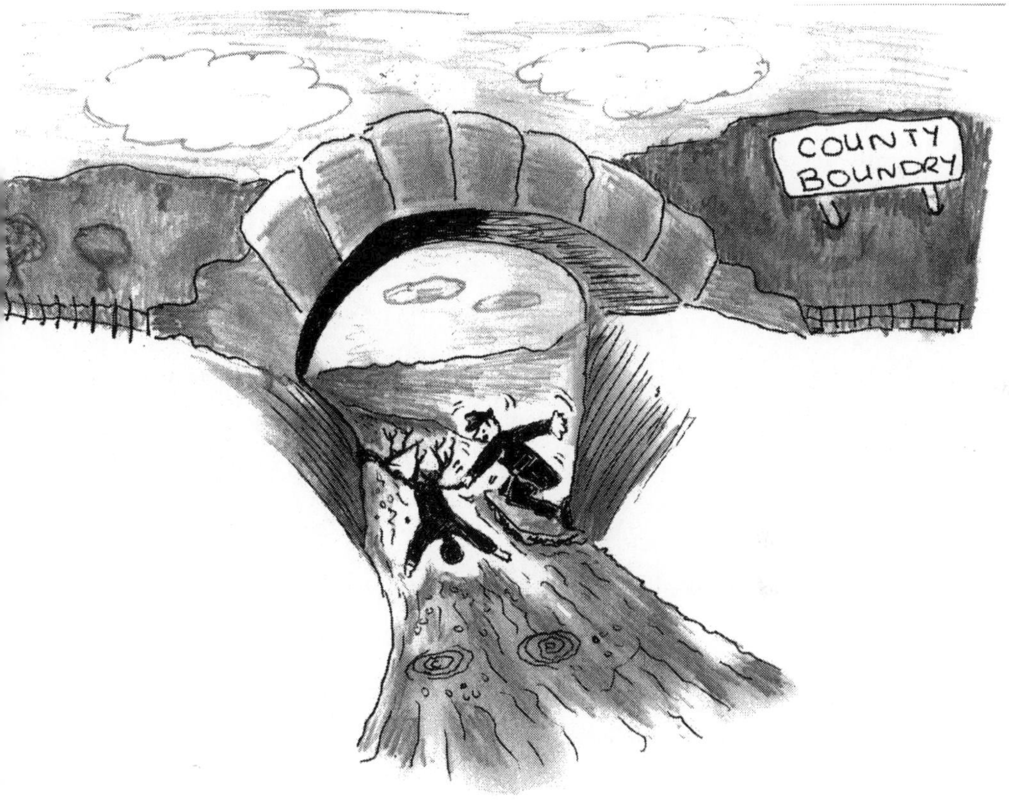
COUNTY
BOUNDRY

THE BLIND AMBULANCE CLEANER

The ageing ambulance cleaner's eyes were so poor that he had to wear thick 'bottle-end glasses' to aid his blurred vision. Although he still drove his Austin Seven to and from work, he only knew he had arrived at his ambulance parking spot when his car's bumper touched the wall. He use to guess which ambulances needed cleaning by feeling the vehicle with his hands. If it felt rough to the touch, he would chuck a bucket of water at it.

One day as he drove home from his day of 'uncleaning', police in a marked car spotted the Austin swerving all over the road and suspected the driver must be drunk. They followed him for half a mile before illuminating the blue lights and sounding the horn.

The cleaner, on seeing a faint vision of blue lights through his rear mirror, thought it was the lads playing tricks. The police continued to instruct him to stop, but the cleaner was convinced it was an ambulance crew prank and kept right on going.

When police eventually stopped the 'cleaner', they realised he was virtually blind and booked him for dangerous driving, suspending his licence with immediate effect.

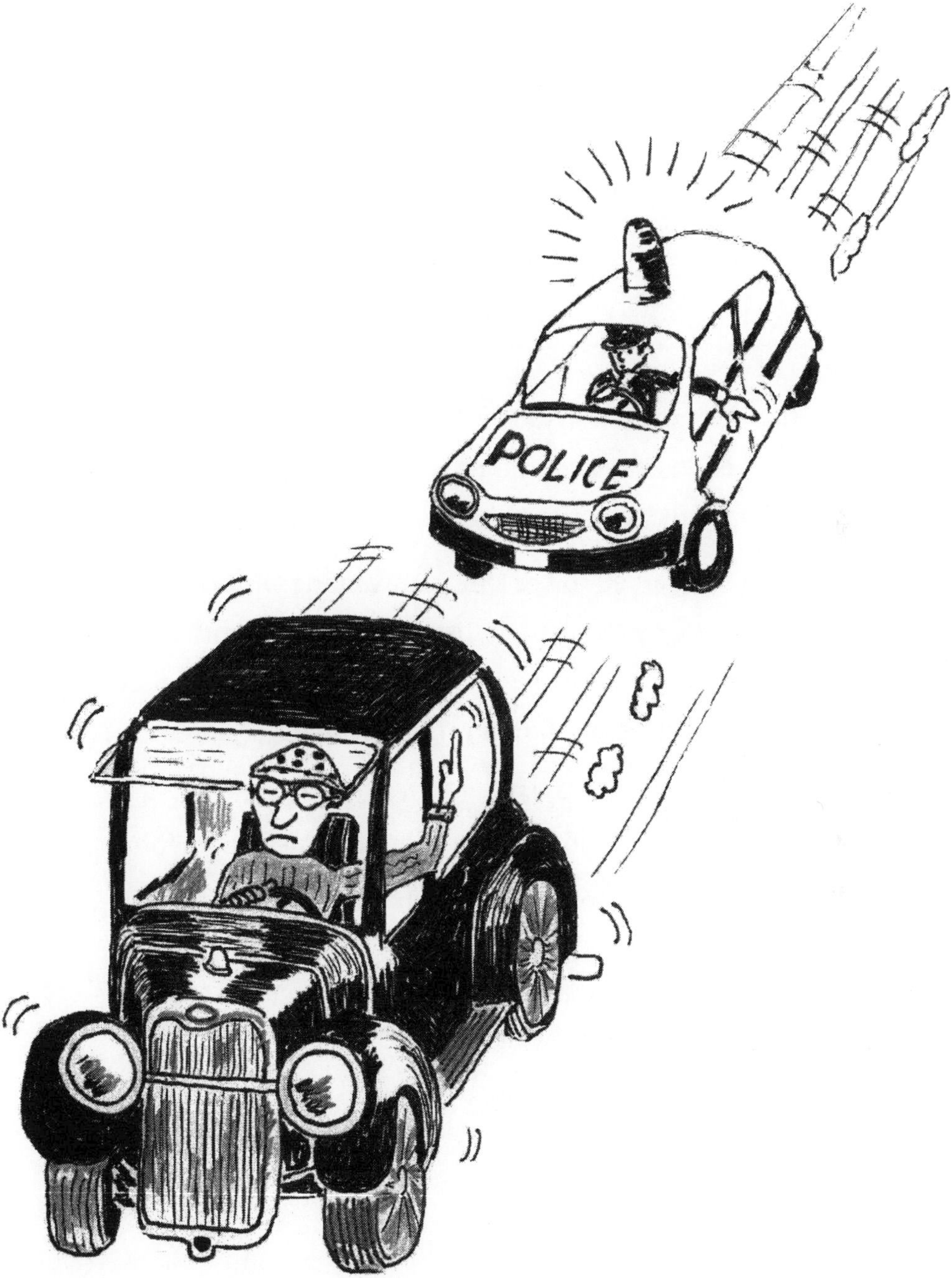
POLICE

AMBULANCE TRANSFER, SIR?

Not only were ambulance staff on very poor wages in the sixties, but uniforms were hard to come by. One ambulance man had still not been issued with a uniform after more than two years. Instead a fireman had given him a very smart double-breasted dark uniform jacket, with lots of silver buttons.

This uniform worked to the crew's advantage when dealing with a particularly awkward patient. A hospital transfer was about to be assigned for an elderly senile male who wouldn't cooperate with any of the nurses.

The ambulance man explained, 'When I went in to see the patient in the cubicle in my smart double-breasted uniform with silver buttons and my shiny cap, the old chap took one look at me, leapt to his feet and shouted '123468 Brown sir!' and saluted. It turned out that he had been in the Navy and thought I was a Petty Officer.

'I told him to get his kit together and not cause any problems for the nurses, or we would be back to sort him out!'

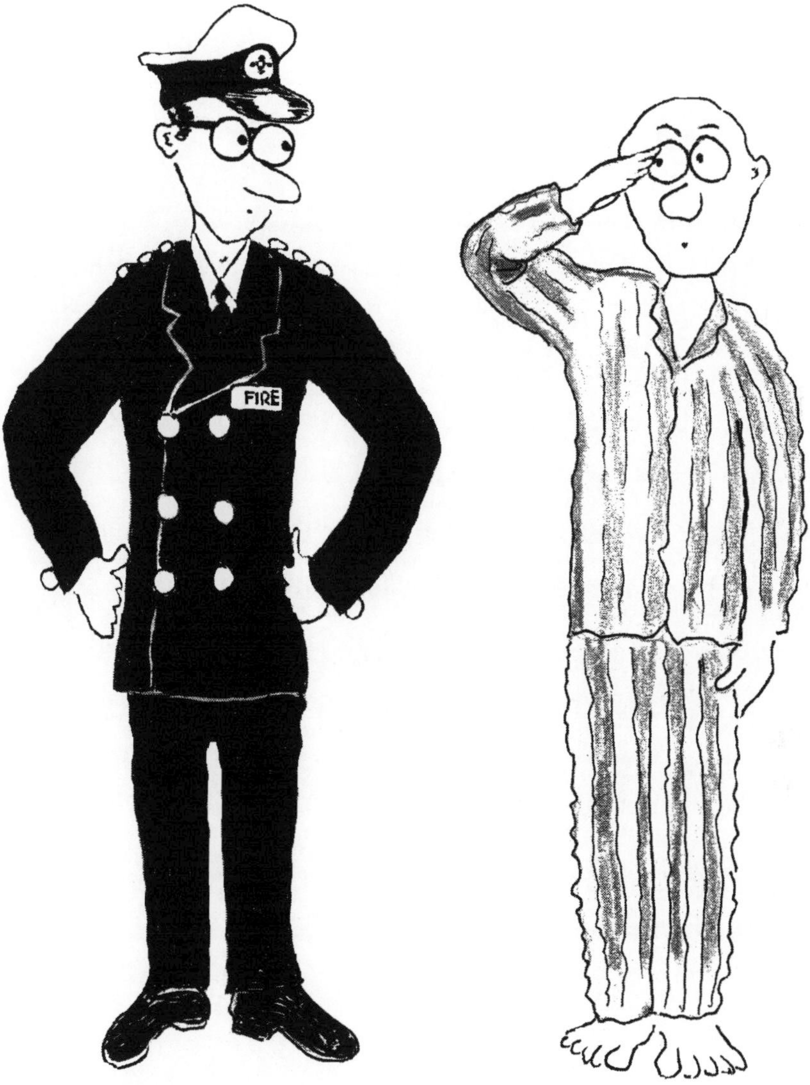
FIRE

ARTHUR, YOU'VE SHRUNK!

The attendant at a road traffic accident (whom we will call Arthur) had a physical handicap and had to wear special stacked shoes to compensate for his club feet. On arrival at the scene, he became overzealous in his desire to help the lorry driver. Without fear of danger, he started running across an unknown spillage to get to his patient.

Arthur failed to realise that the chemical spilt between him and his patient was a shallow film of sulphuric acid.

According to his crew mate, Arthur appeared to be getting smaller as he approached the cab of the lorry. He just about made it to the other side of the road and hurriedly kicked off his boots before the chemical started to burn his feet away.

After the incident, Arthur momentarily thanked his lucky stars for being burdened with the disability that had given him an extra four inches of leather on the soles of his boots and saved his feet from dissolving.

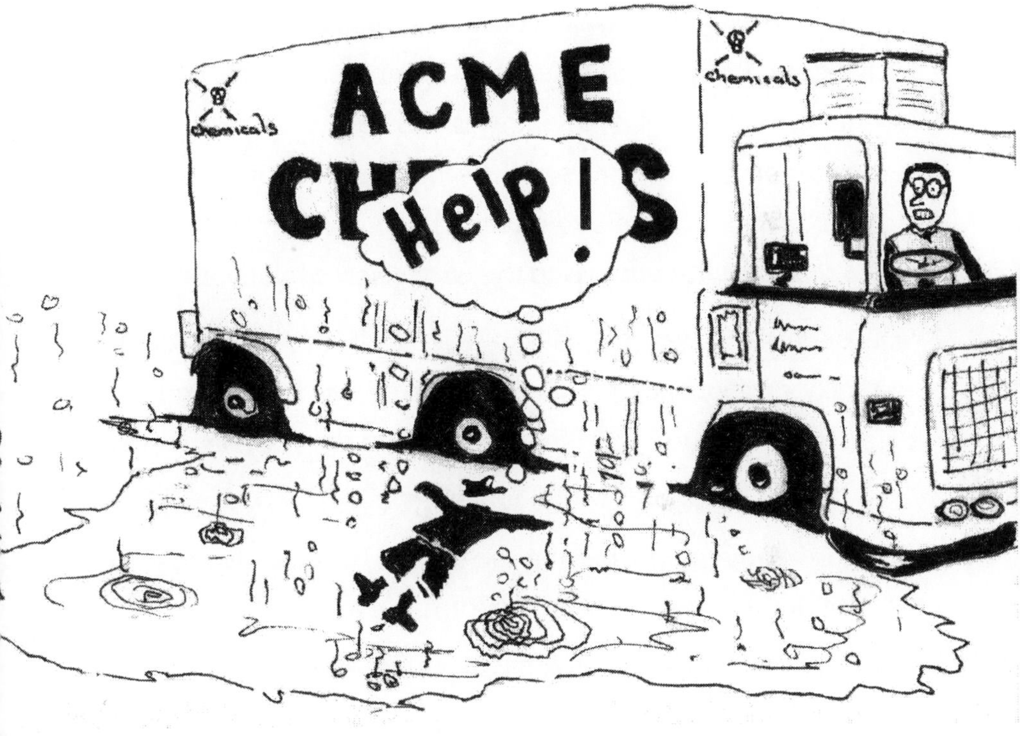
ACME
CH
S
chemicals
chemicals
Help!

It could have been so much worse!!

CERTIFIED ALIVE

When a nursing sister was informed of the death of a patient on a busy night in casualty, she unfortunately got his name confused with that of a patient who was about to be admitted by ambulance. Relatives of the second patient arrived at hospital and were herded into the relative's room as Sister divulged the sad loss to the wrong set of relatives.

This tragic news was met with utter shock from the distraught family, as they had only seen their loved one half an hour before, and she had been fully conscious as she was diagnosed with a grumbling appendix.

As the relatives were leaving the hospital in shock to make their way to the mortuary for formal identification, the ambulance arrived with the real appendix patient, who, after being given gas and air, was feeling much better.

'I bet you hadn't expected to see me looking so well' she said to her shocked relatives. They certainly hadn't.

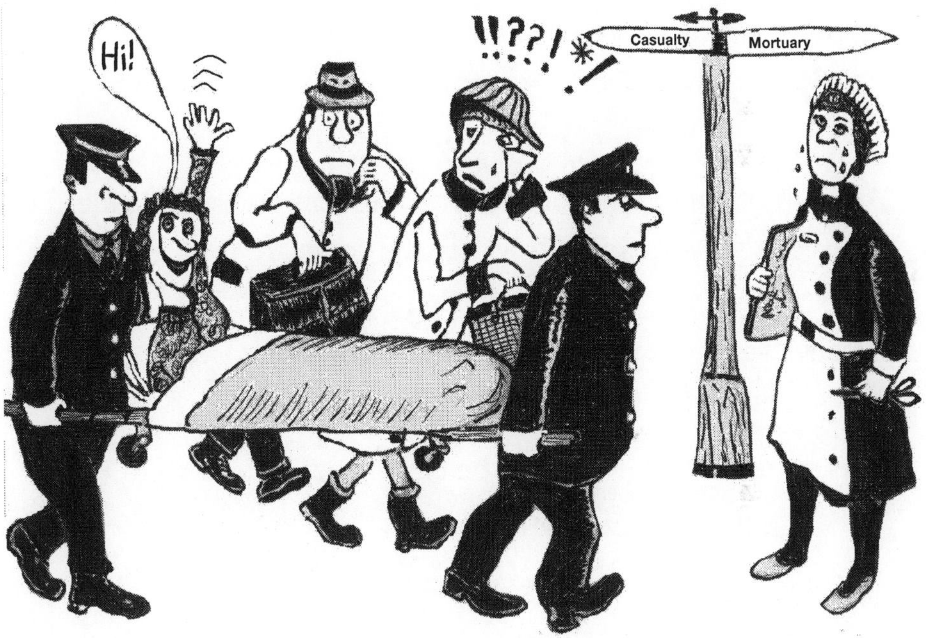
Hi!
!!??!*!
Casualty
Mortuary

BACK FROM THE DEAD

Ambulance control passed a case to a crew as 'man dead in bed.' When the crew arrived, they were met by a distraught wife and asked her where her husband was.

'He's in the bedroom' she sobbed. One of the crew stayed with the wife as his mate went to check on the deceased. The crew member consoling the wife started to offer his condolences. Meanwhile his crewmate went to check on the 'deceased' to find him wide awake and sitting bolt upright in bed.

The attendant hurriedly whispered downstairs to his mate, 'He's alive!'

The crewmate consoling the wife quickly changed tack. 'Now I don't want to build your hopes up too high' he said, 'but I think my colleague might have worked his magic!

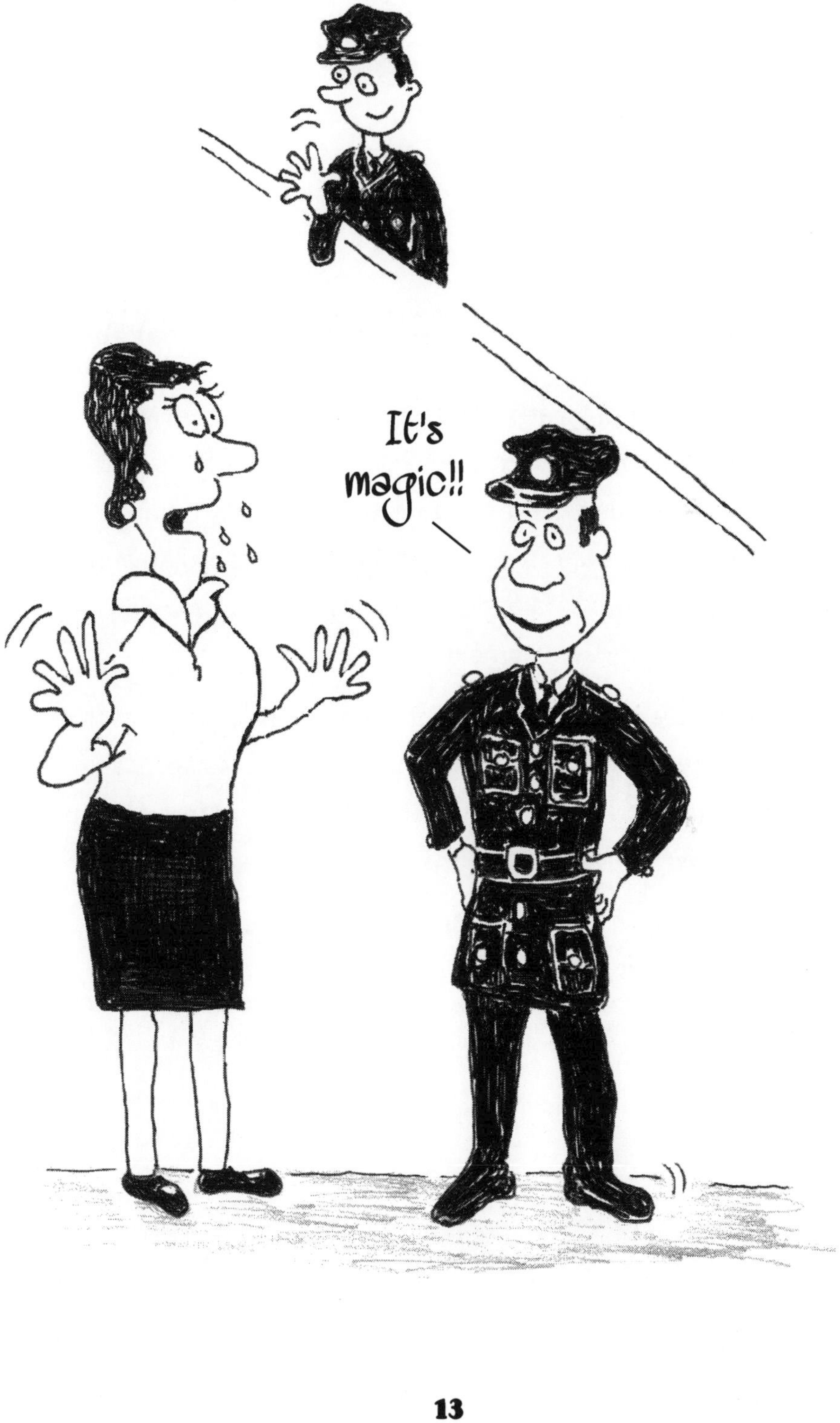
It's magic!!

DON'T COME ANY CLOSER OR ELSE...

The neighbour of an attractive female suffering from manic depression decided to ring 999 because he knew the woman had not been taking her medication and was acting strangely. The ambulance crew arrived to find the patient standing at the front window, skimpily dressed. The crew tried to persuade her to come to hospital.

It was then she shouted out one of the most bizarre threats the crew had ever heard. 'I'm warning you, for every step closer you come towards me I will take off an item of clothing, and I'm not joking' she said.

As the ambulance attendant said, 'I had to approach her, in the interests of her own safety.' That was his story and he was sticking to it.

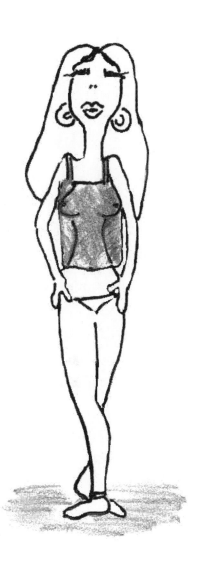

FAMILY VALUES

A leading ambulance man told the crew to go and investigate the report of an elderly deceased female. The station coffin was placed on the ambulance and off they went.

On arrival, a neighbour led the crew into a front room, where the dead woman was sitting in a chair. Although it was a warm day, her curtains were still drawn and her TV and gas fire were still on. The crew said she must have been dead for days.

The body was placed in the coffin, certified deceased at casualty and taken to the mortuary. On return to the ambulance station, the leading ambulance man who had sent them on the case was curious about the circumstances. After hearing their story, he remarked 'You know, it's disgusting that an old dear like that could be dead for so long without any input from her family, what's wrong with relatives today'?

After the ambulance man completed his incident form, he handed it in to leading ambulance man, who gasped 'Oh my God, it's my mother-in-law!'

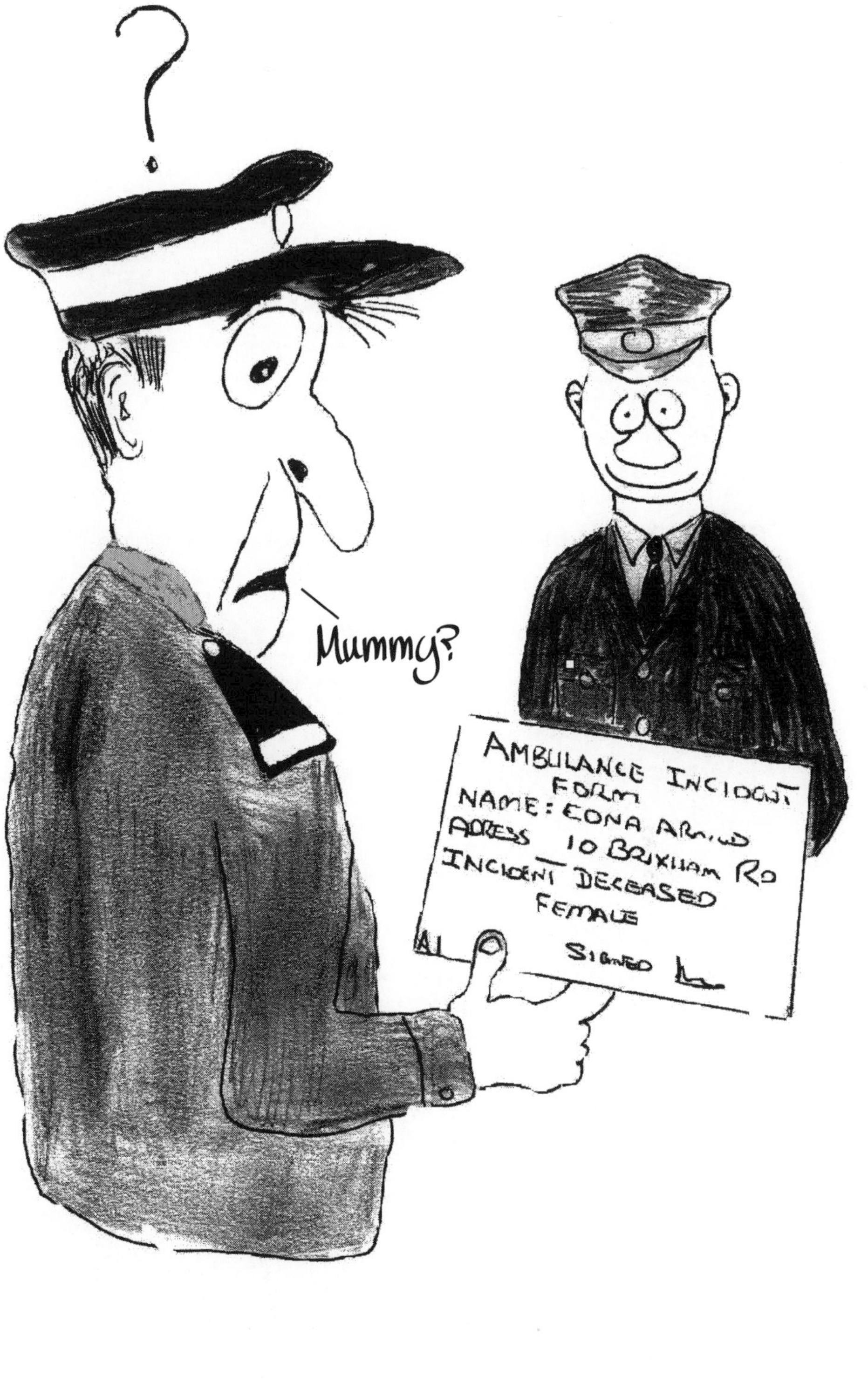
Mummy?
AMBULANCE INCIDENT FORM
NAME: EDNA ARNOLD
ADRESS 10 BRIXHAM RD
INCIDENT DECEASED FEMALE
SIGNED

HEAVY BREATHING

After assessing a patient in the rear of his vehicle, a trainee decided to place an oxygen mask around the patient's face. The drive to hospital began.

On the way, the ambulance driver heard loud hissing noises coming from the rear of the vehicle, followed by gasps for breath. Thinking the patient's condition was deteriorating, the driver began to accelerate, but a quick look in his rear-view mirror revealed that the sounds were coming from the trainee. He was making loud hissing sounds through his teeth, then going blue in the face and giving an enormous gasp for breath before the next loud hissing noise started.

Yet another shortfall had been exposed - he didn't know how to turn the oxygen on, and rather than ask, he decided to simulate the sound of the flowing of oxygen by hissing through his teeth.

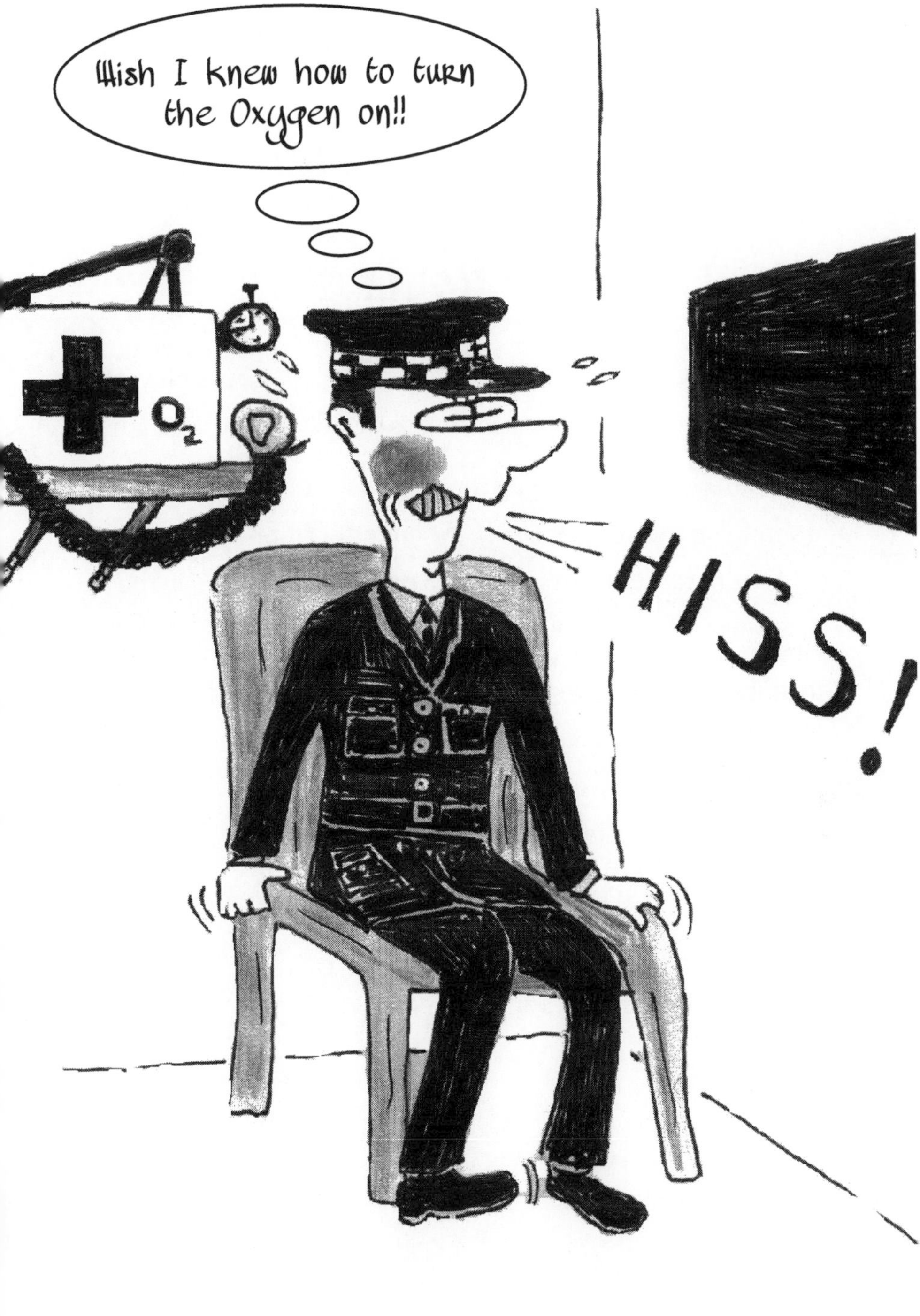
Wish I knew how to turn the Oxygen on!!
O2
HISS!

GIVE YOURSELF UP!

An ex-soldier was threatening to commit suicide because his wife had left him. An ambulance was sent, as no police were available.

On arrival, the crew walked up the stairs and could see a young man sitting on the edge of a bed. When they climbed closer they could see that the lad was holding a gun and pointing it in the direction of the crew.

Both ambulance men jumped back downstairs several steps at a time. Trembling with fear, they muttered to each other 'what shall we do now? Do we do the right thing and call out the Police and Army gun squad'?

Instead they decided to use their own initiative. They shouted up stairs 'Come out, you're surrounded! throw away your gun now!'

To the crew's amazement, he did so.

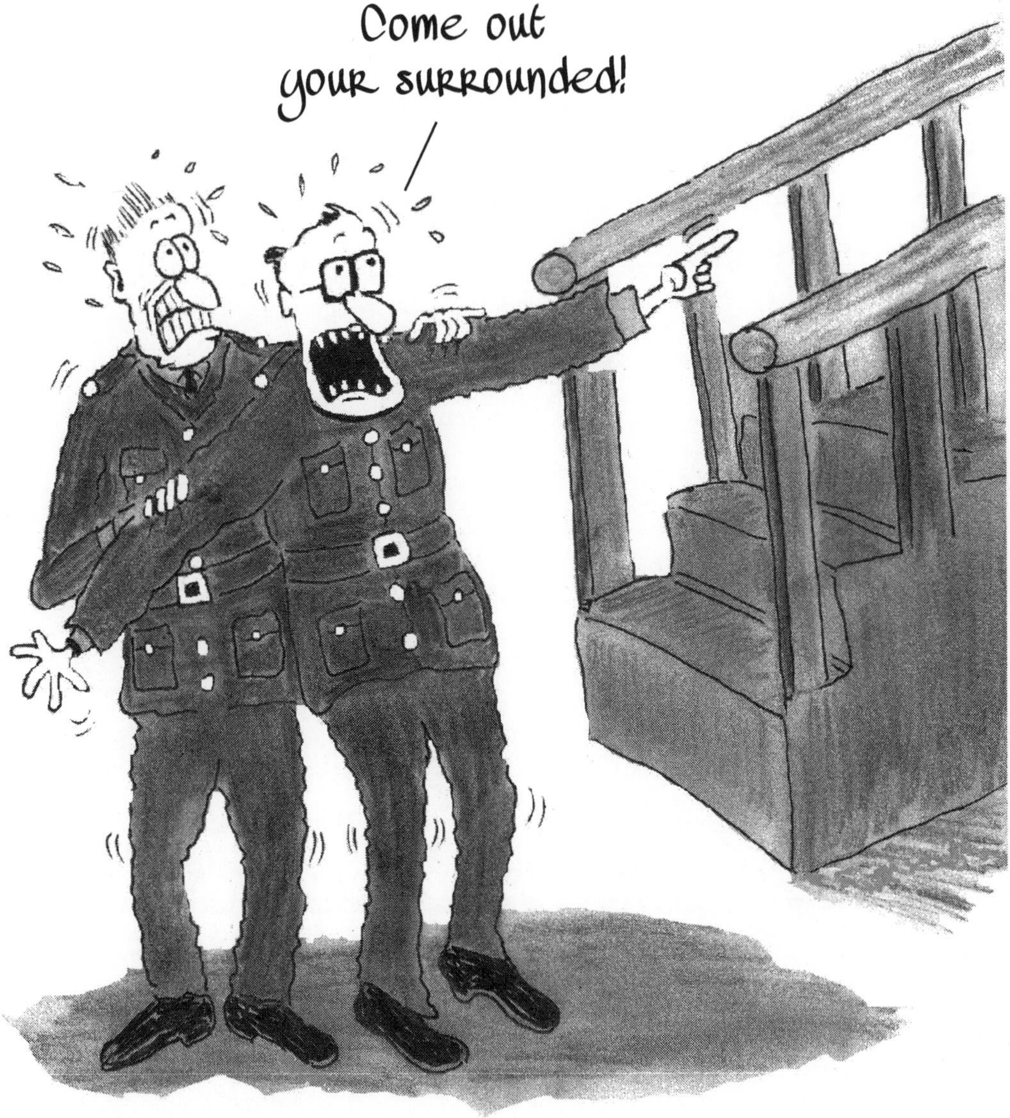
Come out
your surrounded!

GYNAECOLOGY IN THE 1960S

The ambulance crew was met at the door by a husband who had been playing out a sexual fantasy scene in the bedroom. He had inserted a pear-shaped perfume bottle into his wife's vagina and lost hold of it. She was naturally extremely annoyed.

The crew decided (with the wife's permission) to extract the bottle by using artery forceps, clamps, rubber gloves and gas and air to relax her.

After a considerable amount of grunting and groaning, the perfume bottle was eventually removed.

The wife was overwhelmed. She shouted out erotically 'Oooh, you men certainly know your stuff!'

Back in the ambulance, the attendant said, 'Blimey, I didn't even get to know her name, what am I going to put on the form?'

His mate answered 'I don't bloody know, you were the one in bed with her!'

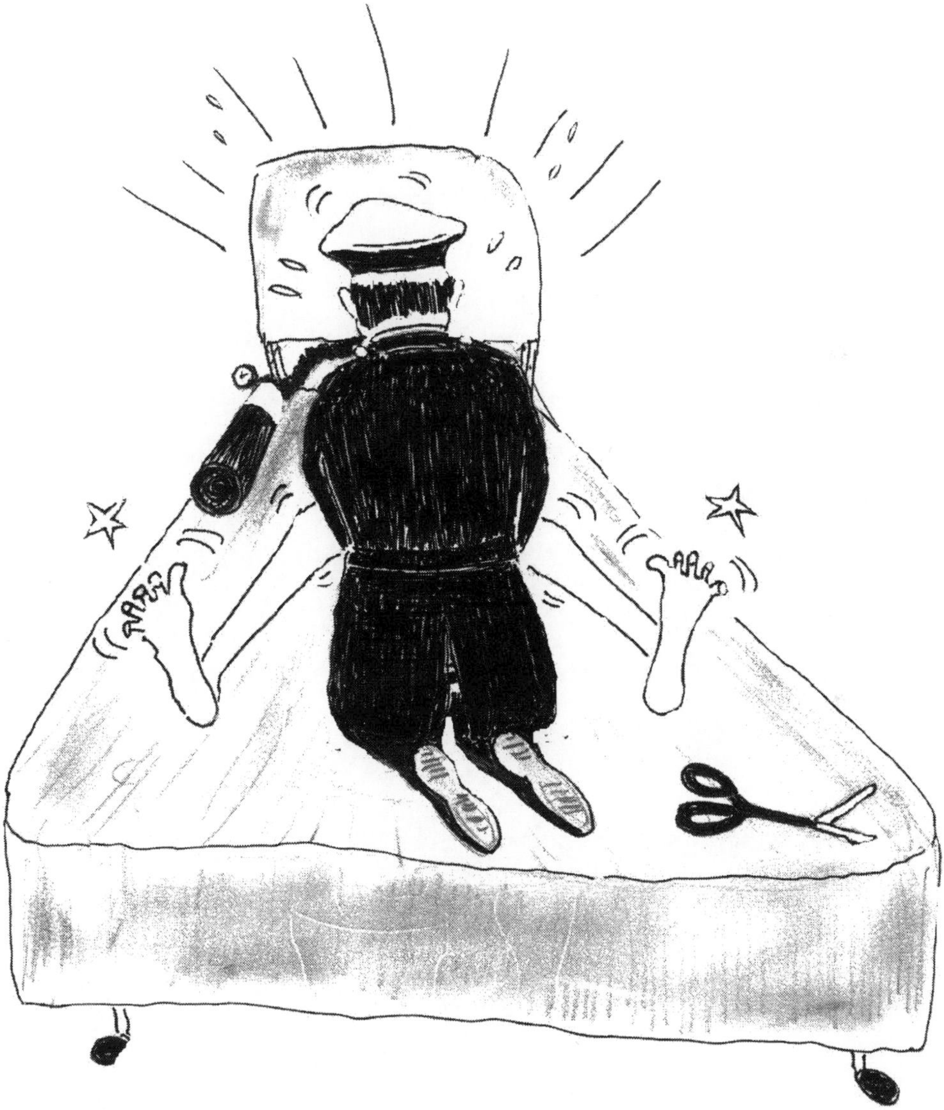

THE CORPSE WHO WANTED A CUPPA

An ambulance crew was called in the middle of the night to the report of a male collapsed, believed to be deceased. They found the man lying in his bed and of moribund appearance.

Crews in those days had no monitors or stethoscopes to rely on and officially were not allowed to confirm death. However, the family were expecting some confirmation from the crew that their worst fears were correct.

The crew came downstairs and uttered the sad words in what was commonly known as 'funeral director mode' that he had indeed passed on.

They had just finished breaking the news that their loved one had passed on to a better place when the corpse wandered downstairs, went into the kitchen and made himself a cup of tea.

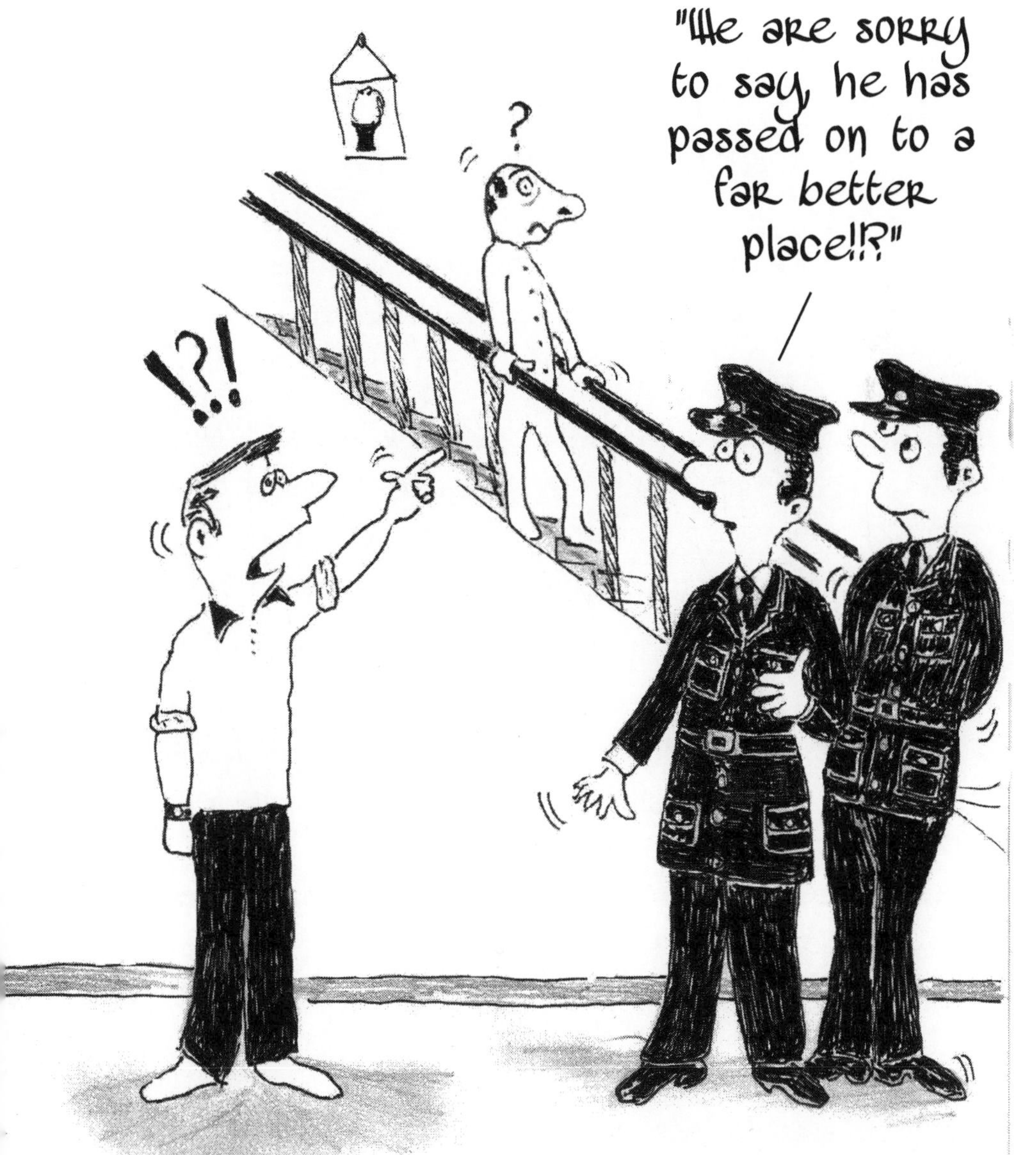
"We are sorry to say, he has passed on to a far better place!!?"
?
!?!

DEAD MAN'S GNASHERS

An ambulance man was moaning because of his ill-fitting dentures. His crewmate asked to have a look to see what size they were.

His mate was somewhat dismayed at this, as he didn't realise dentures were sized. His friend said, 'Take your teeth out and look at the veins at the back of the plate, which make a number. Yours is a number 4 and I think you need a number 1'.

In the afternoon, his crewmate acquired a number 1 set, convincing his crew mate that the veins on the plate made numbers. 'Try these' he said. As his mate put the new falsies into his mouth, he complained that they were still a little bit loose.

His crewmate replied 'Well, I can't believe that, because Eric the mortician assured me they would fit.'

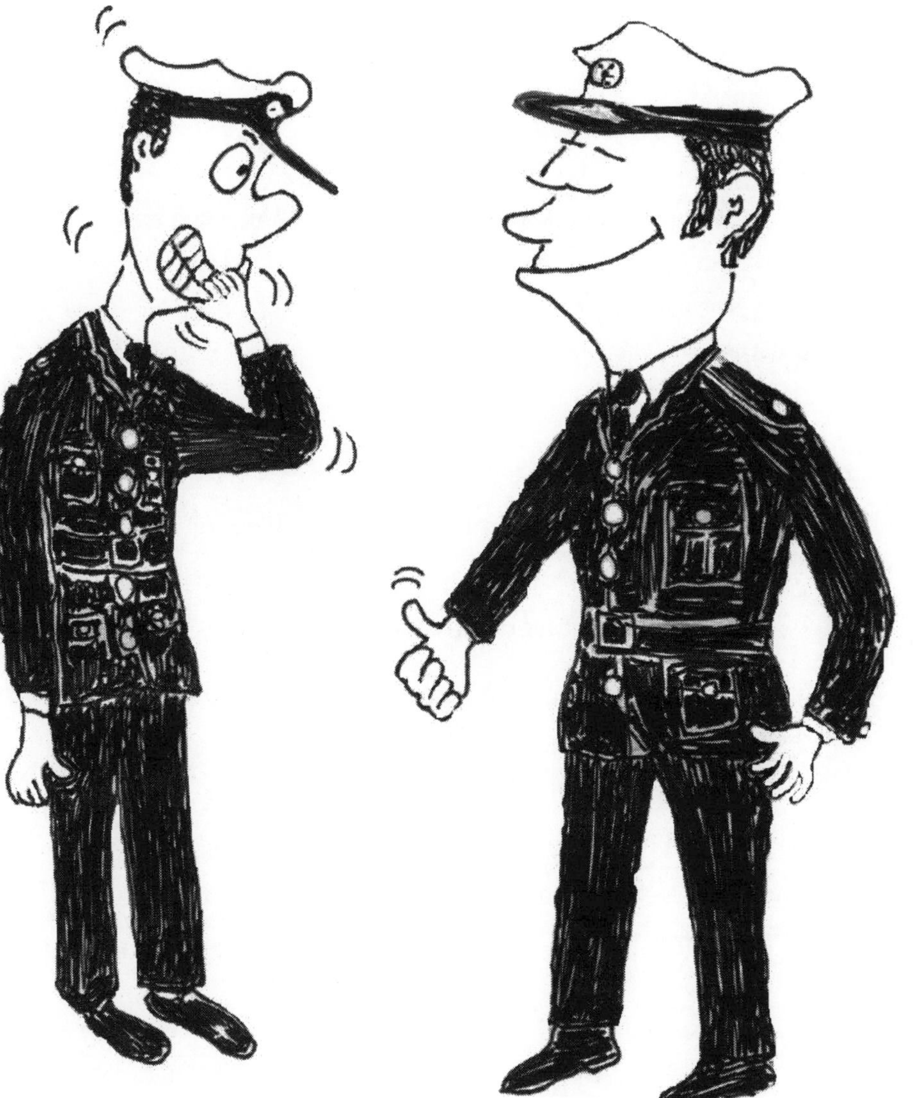

A QUESTION OF PRIORITIES

When the ambulance arrived at a collapse case, the crew entered the house to attend to the patient. After a quick check of the pulse (to make sure he had one), they put the patient on oxygen and decided to take him to hospital for a check-up.

The more senior crew member instructed his junior colleague to return to the ambulance and bring back a carry chair. The senior man stayed with the patient and waited.

15 minutes passed with no sign of the chair. Eventually the senior man left his patient to see what had happened to his junior, only to find him in next door's Post Office, waiting in a queue and trying to pay his gas bill. When challenged, he answered, 'Well, the patient didn't seem to be too serious and my gas bill was well overdue, so I decided to prioritise.'

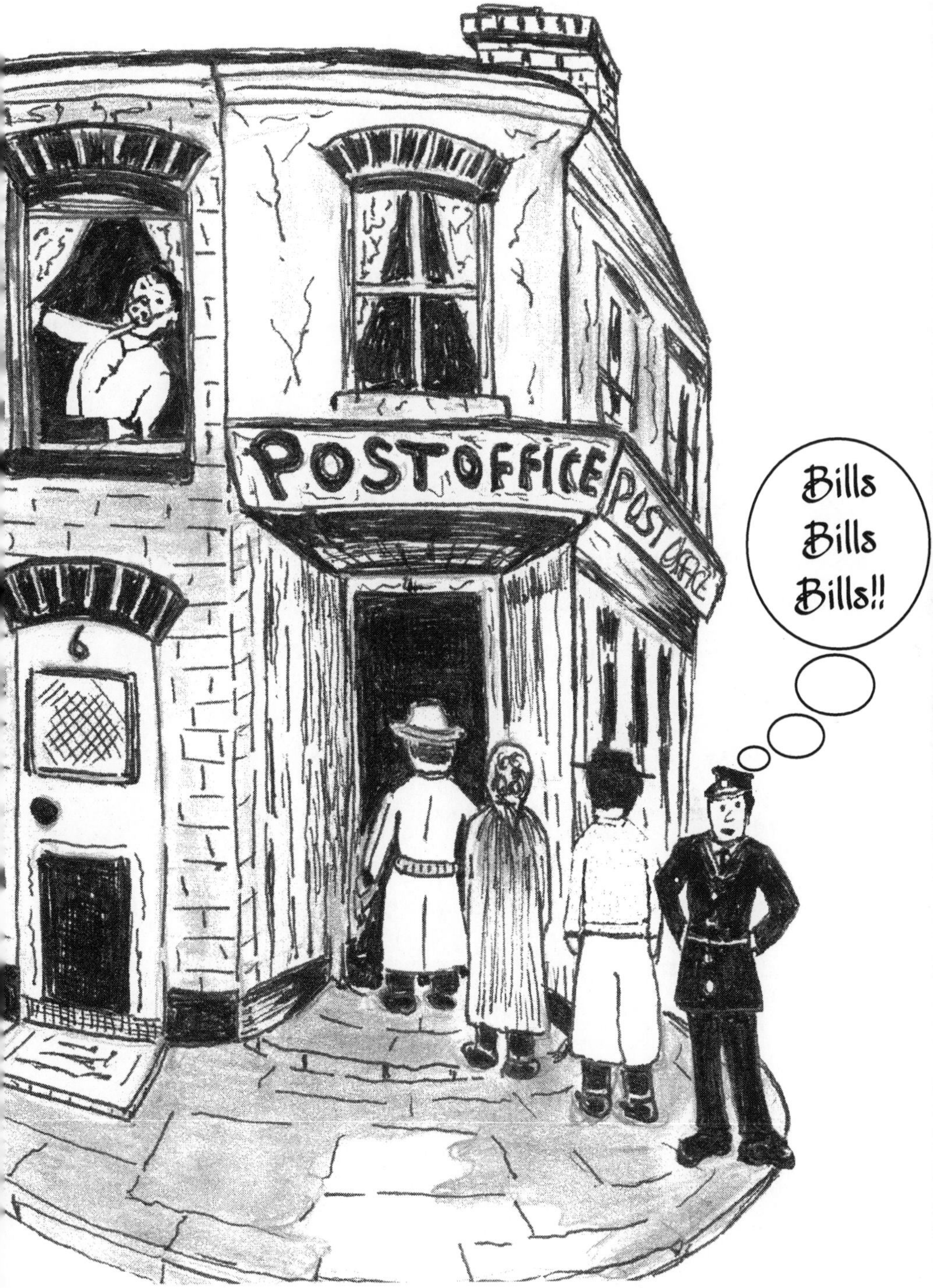
POSTOFFICE
POST OFFICE
Bills
Bills
Bills!!

I'VE GOT A BONE TO PICK WITH YOU...

While on their travels, an ambulance crew came across a plastic toy skull in a disused car park. They placed it on a pillow at the head of the stretcher, rolled up six blankets to simulate a body, covered them with a red blanket and rang Sister at Casualty, saying they had come across a patient in a very poor condition and were coming into A&E for an assessment.

As they ran into Casualty with their 'patient', the joke soon backfired.

The look on Sister's face was one of horror. Not because she didn't enjoy a joke, but because she had put a resus team on standby, including a registrar, who had been pulled out of theatre to direct proceedings.

Much to the acute embarrassment of the crew.

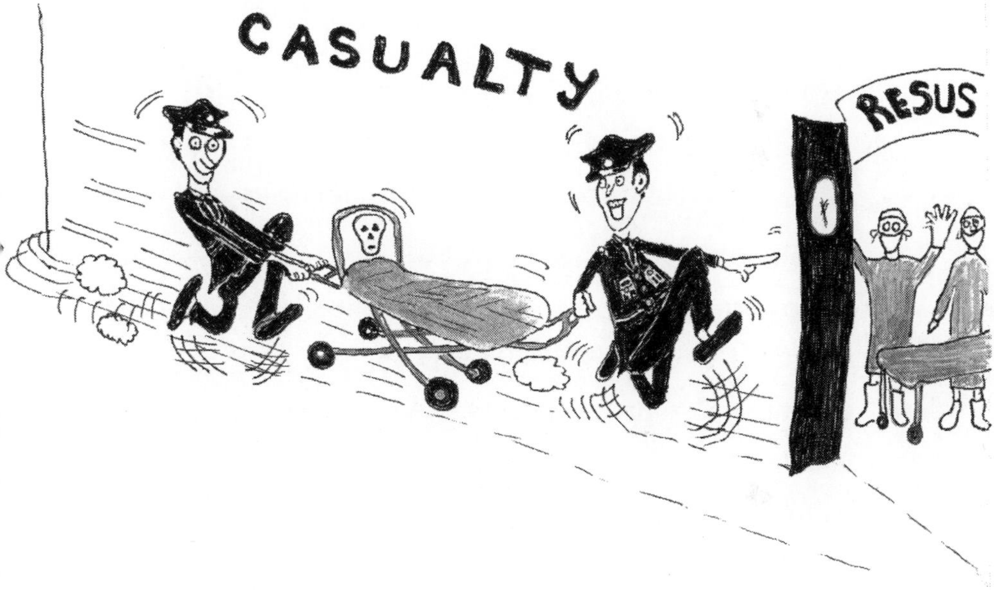
CASUALTY
RESUS

THE EXPLODING TOILET

An ambulance was called to the report of an explosion in a factory. On arrival they found the patient in the gents and asked him to explain what had happened.

'I was waiting outside the toilet' he said. 'Unknown to me, the person occupying the cubicle before me had poured the remains of five pints of traffic film remover down the toilet and didn't pull the chain. As I sat down on the toilet seat, I removed my newspaper from my back pocket and lit my cigarette. I threw the match into the toilet, causing an almighty explosion, which blew me clean out of the trap. And then you lot turned up!'

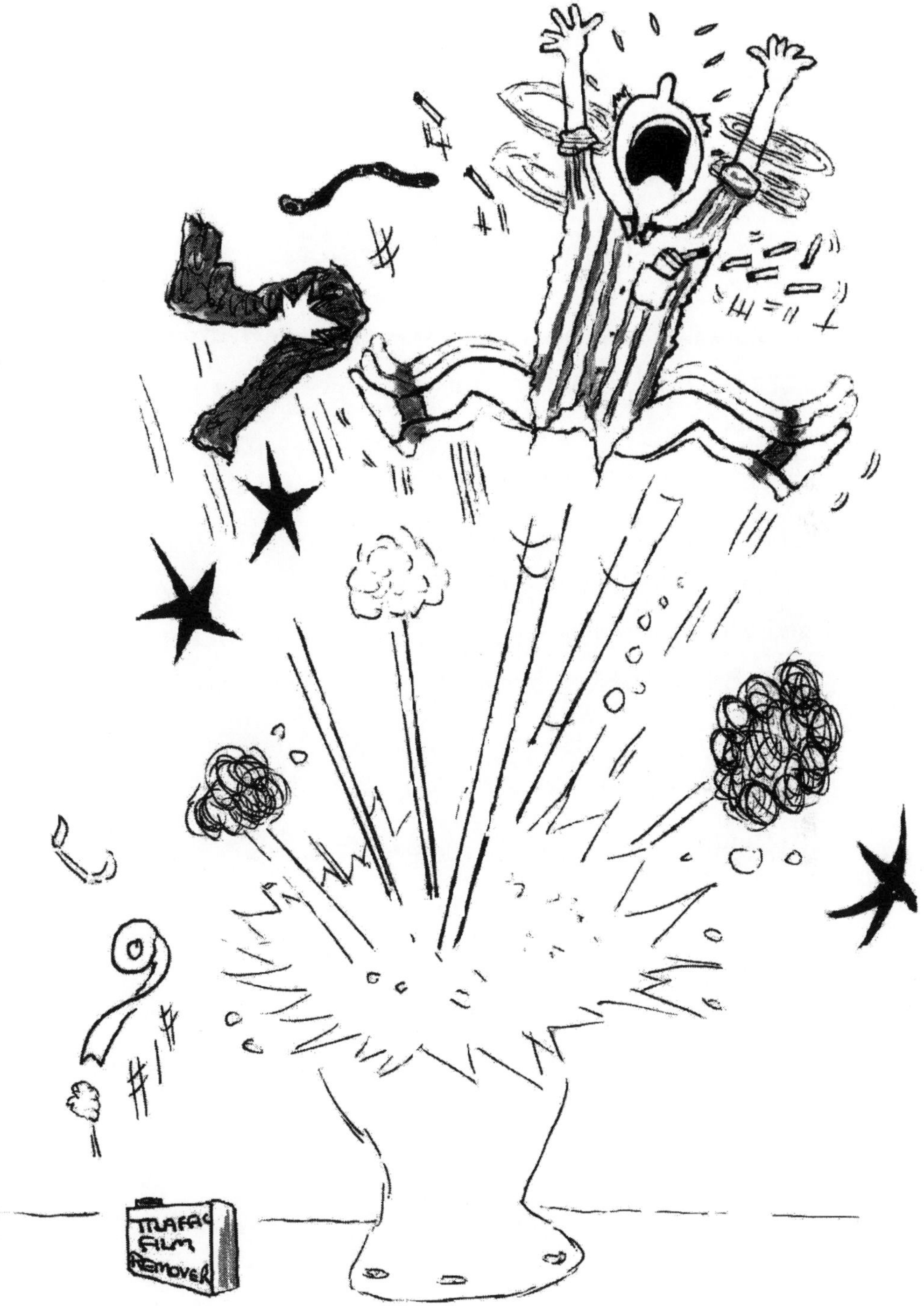
TRAFFIC
FILM
REMOVER

A STIFF PROBLEM

After attending an obviously-deceased patient on the 14th floor of a high-rise block of flats, the ambulance crew were in a quandary, wondering how to transport the body to hospital for certification of death.

The body had been found in a disused communal TV lounge and due to rigor mortis, was as stiff as a board. The deceased wouldn't be able to sit on a chair, because he couldn't bend. A stretcher was out of the question, because the lift was not wide enough.

The crew decided to stand the deceased upright. By sandwiching the body between them, they walked it into the lift.

On descent, the lift stopped on every floor. As people got in and out, the ambulance men started to throw their voices to mask the fact the patient was dead.

'So you've had a good night out then?' said one of the ambulance men. 'Yes thanks' said his crew mate, answering back like a ventriloquist. 'But I could do with a stiff drink!'

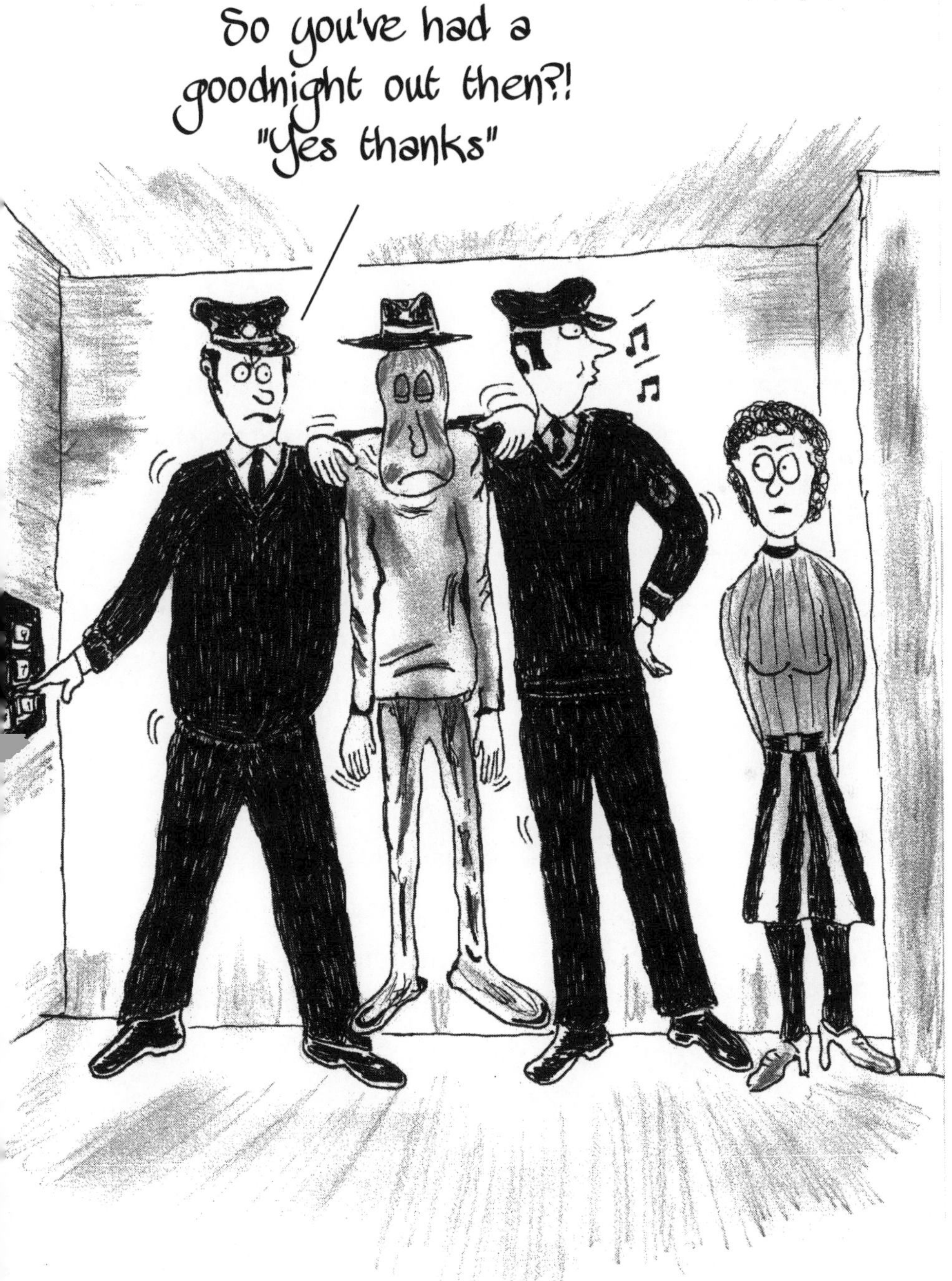
So you've had a goodnight out then?!
"Yes thanks"

LITTLE AND LARGE

Alex and Bert had been crewmates for nearly 20 years. Alex was six feet tall with a pot belly, while his mate Bert was four foot nothing and skeletal in appearance. On nights, between jobs, the pair would strip off to their vests and pants, take out their false teeth and occupy a stretcher each in the back of their vehicle.

On one occasion, Bert and Alex were snoring their heads off as two of their shiftmates crept into their vehicle, switched the two sets of uniforms and false teeth and left them to wait for their next emergency call.

When the bells rang at 3 am, Alex and Bert struggled out of their pits. Both men pulled on the wrong uniforms and placed the wrong false teeth in their mouths. Alex looked like Billy Bunter in short trousers, and his vertically-challenged crew mate was tripping over his colleagues enormous pants. The crew were desperately trying to answer the voice radio message from control, both sounding as if they had suffered some sort of seizure.

WRONG ADDRESS

An ambulance was sent to investigate the plight of a lady who was reported to have fallen over in the front room of a mid-terraced house. On arrival, they could see the patient lying on the floor in some distress.

They attempted to gain access by trying to break in through the front, but the door was immoveable. Instead they made their way to the rear of the property and decided to break in through the back by smashing their way directly into a kitchen area. Here they found a man and wife having their tea.

It was then and only then that they realised they had broken into the wrong house.

TASTY NUTS, ONE PREVIOUS OWNER

A regular outpatient loved her ambulance trips to and from the diabetic clinic so much that she always asked to be dropped off last, so she could enjoy the longer ride home. This request was always granted, and on completion of her journey our lovely old lady would offer one of her special treats before saying her goodbyes.

These treats would normally be in a bowl on the sideboard and usually consisted of hazel nuts. It was rude to refuse, as this might offend, so week after week the crew accepted the nuts as her thank you, until one day the old lady revealed where they were coming from.

'I know I shouldn't eat the chocolate, because of my diabetes, but at least I don't have to worry about my nut allergy' she said.

Suddenly, realisation set in. The hazel nuts were the sucked-off remains of chocolate whole-nut bars. That was the last time they sampled the lady's free nuts.

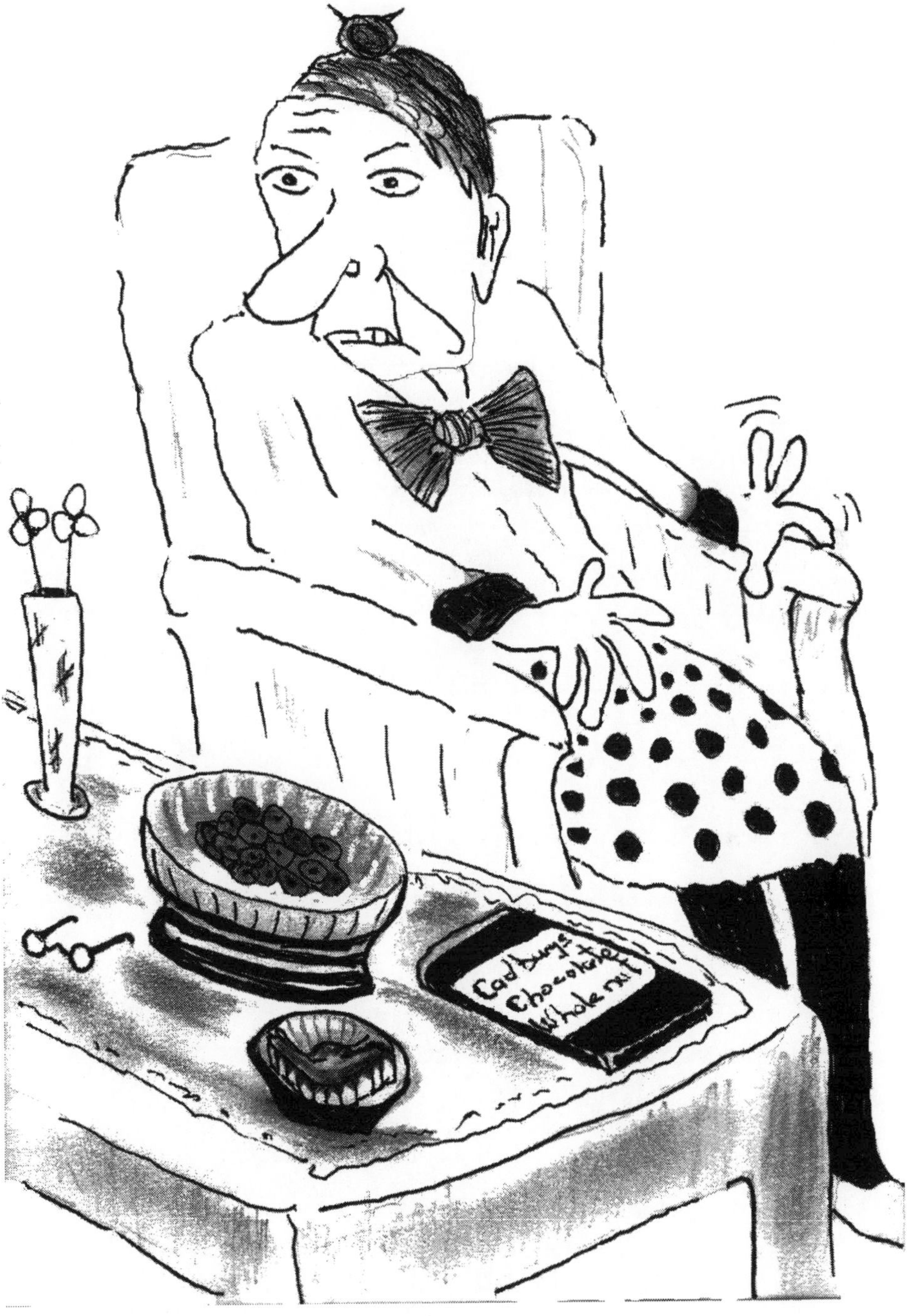
Cadburys
Chocolate
Whole nut

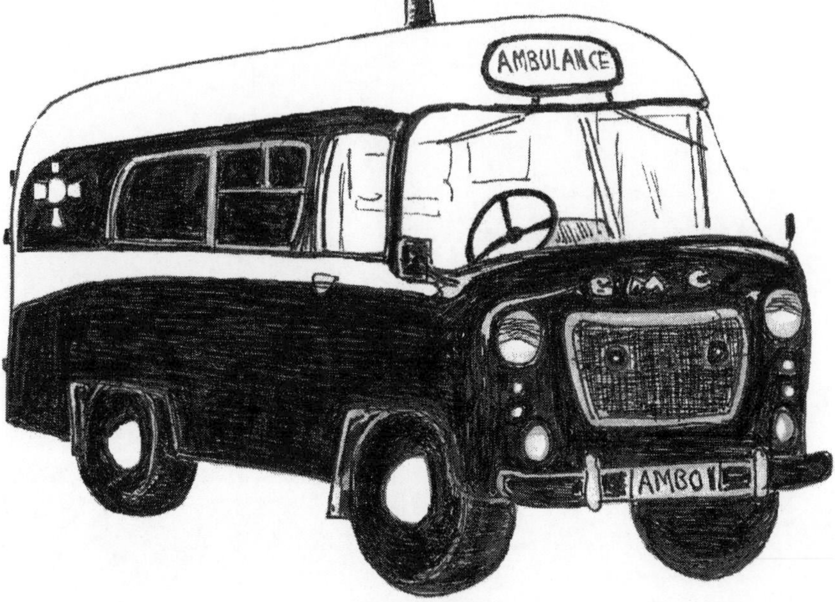
AMBULANCE

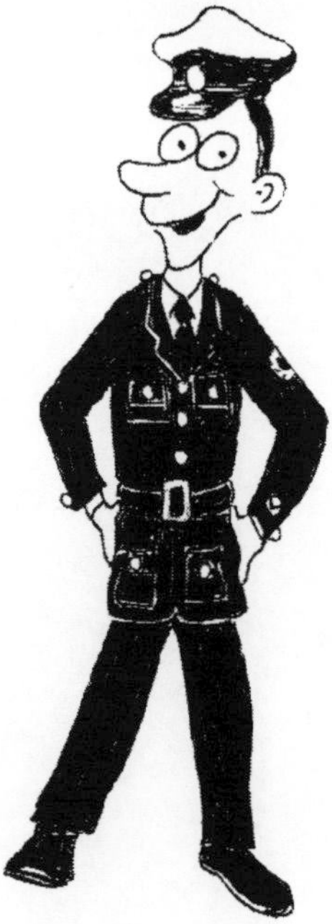

THE 1970'S

SPIN DOCTOR

ABSOLUTELY LEGLESS

BACK FROM THE GRAVE

INSTANT RESPONSE

YOU'RE A WIDOW, HAPPY NEW YEAR

SEEN IT ALL BEFORE

ONE SMALL STEP FOR MANKIND

OWN GOAL

DESPERATE FOR THE LOO

JUST POUR IT BACK IN, DEAR

SNOW WHITE AND THE SIX DWARFS

AN ARMLESS BIT OF CONFUSION

THE WRONG HANDBAG

SHAME TO WASTE IT...

NARROW ESCAPE

DOORS CLOSING...

APPOINTMENT WITH DEATH

TECHNOSPEAK

WALKIES!

LOST ON THE A45

SPIN DOCTOR

In the early 70s, media relations in the ambulance service was run on an amateur basis. Anyone who fancied standing up and having a go at making a statement on behalf of the ambulance service could do so.

This all changed after certain members of staff showed a lack of diplomacy in conveying the correct corporate message. It was very clearly demonstrated when on live radio one day an ambulance man was asked about the clinical condition of a patient he had attended to after a road traffic accident.

"The patient's heart was going like the clappers and he was bleeding like a stuck pig" he replied.

Not quite the sort of statement the reporters had expected.

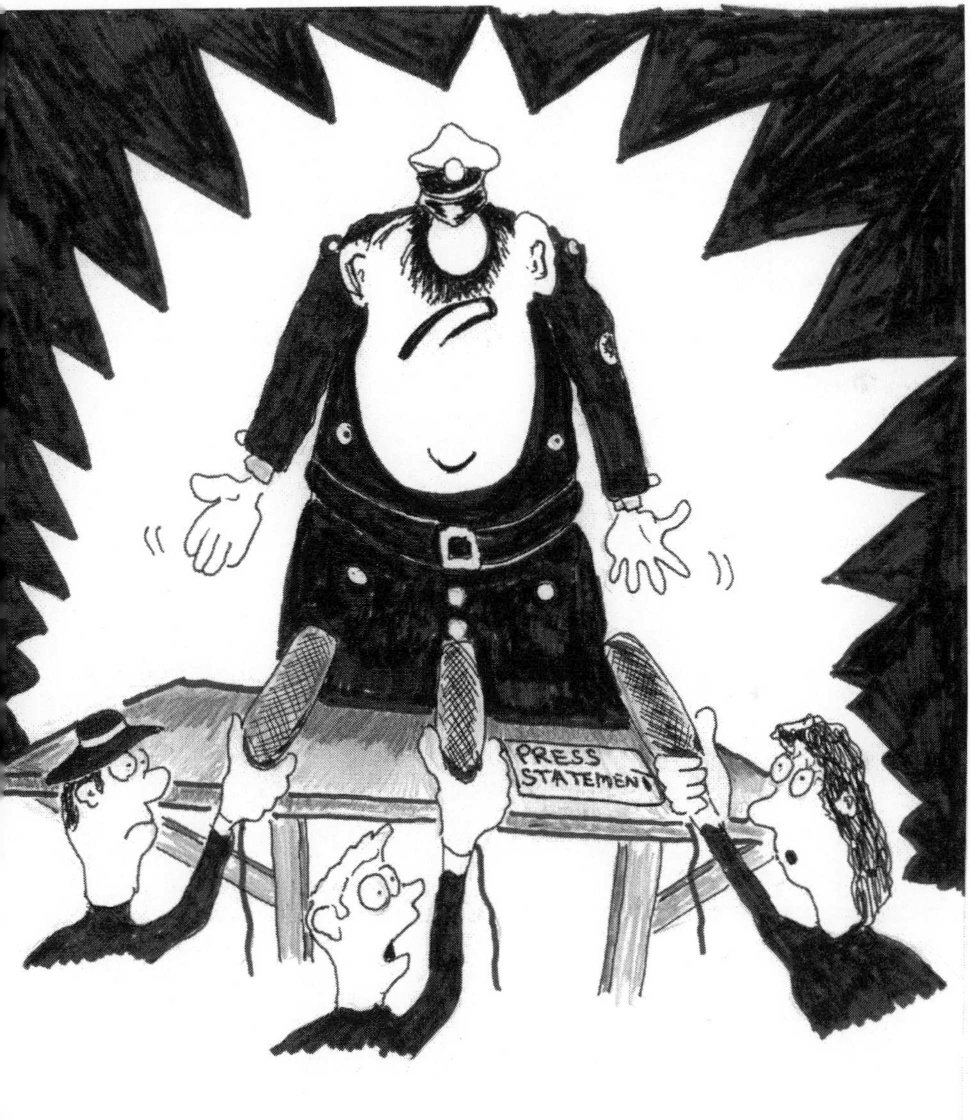
PRESS
STATEMENT

ABSOLUTELY LEGLESS

When a crew attended a road traffic accident on a motorway, the lorry driver told them he had fallen asleep behind the wheel before crashing down the embankment. The driver smelled of alcohol as he limped up the embankment and into the ambulance. He had been very lucky to escape injury.

The police officer asked the ambulance crew if there were any obvious injuries and the crew said there were not.

The lorry driver got on to the stretcher and with slurred speech said 'I'll have to take my artificial leg off, it's killing me.'

When the police officer returned to the ambulance, he took one look at the one-legged driver he said 'Oh my God! I've just told my sergeant he's all right, and his bloody leg's been amputated!'

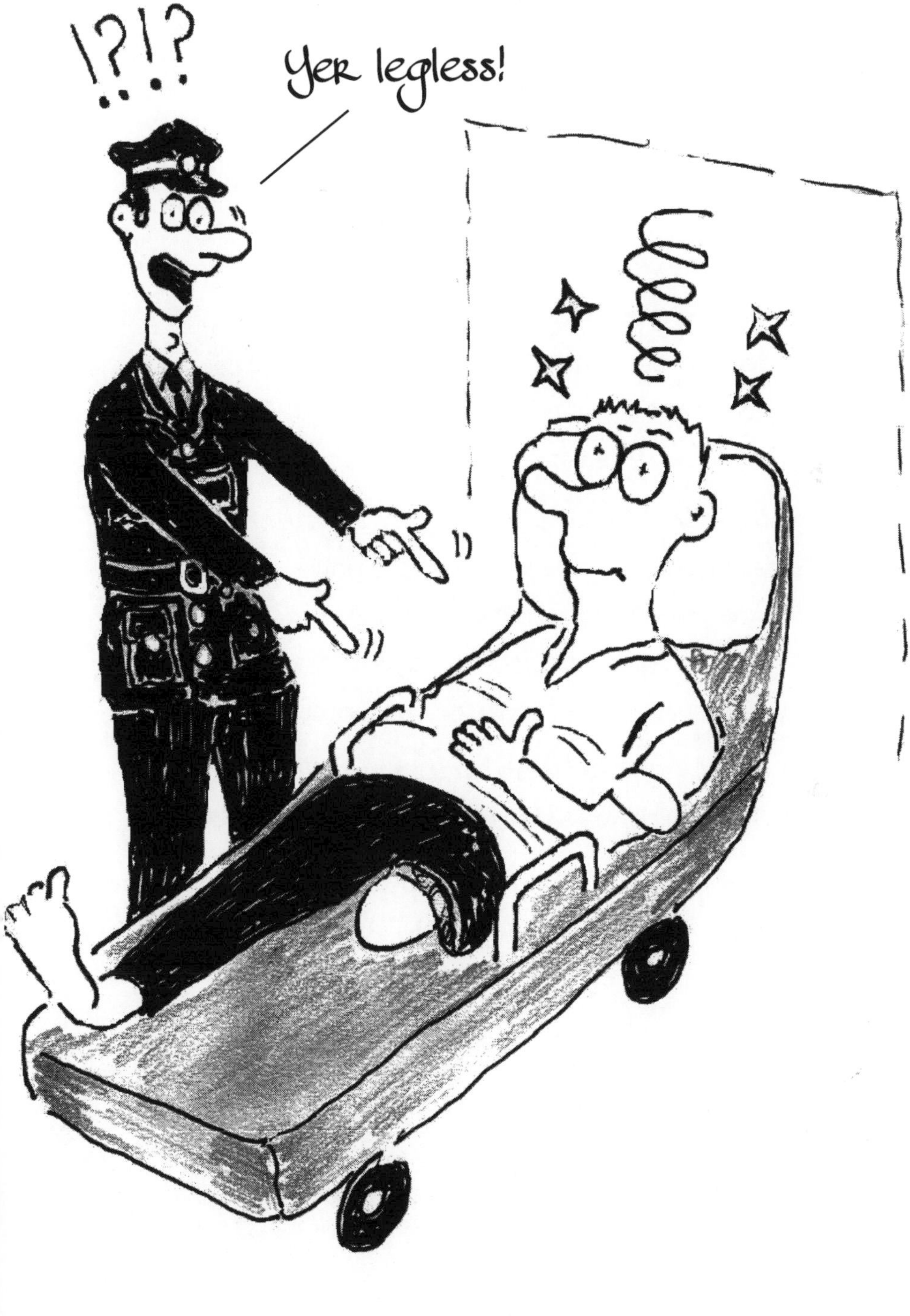
!?!?
Yer legless!

BACK FROM THE GRAVE

A male stroke victim was picked up from casualty to be taken home by ambulance. Because of the patient's previous history, he was booked as a two-man lift. He lived in a block of flats on the outskirts of the city, but there was a query as to which block he actually lived in, as they all looked the same.

Unfortunately the patient couldn't help the crew, because his stroke had taken away his ability to speak. However, they thought they knew which high-rise it was. On arrival at the flats, the patient appeared to indicate his block by raising his arm, so he was wheeled up to the front entrance.

The ambulance man pressed the button of the flat number. Eventually a lady answered the intercom and said 'Hello, who is it?'

'It's the ambulance service' replied the crew. 'We've brought home your better half'.

There was silence for at least a minute before the lady finally replied 'You'd have a job. He's been dead for 13 years'.

Only then did the crew realise they were at the wrong address.

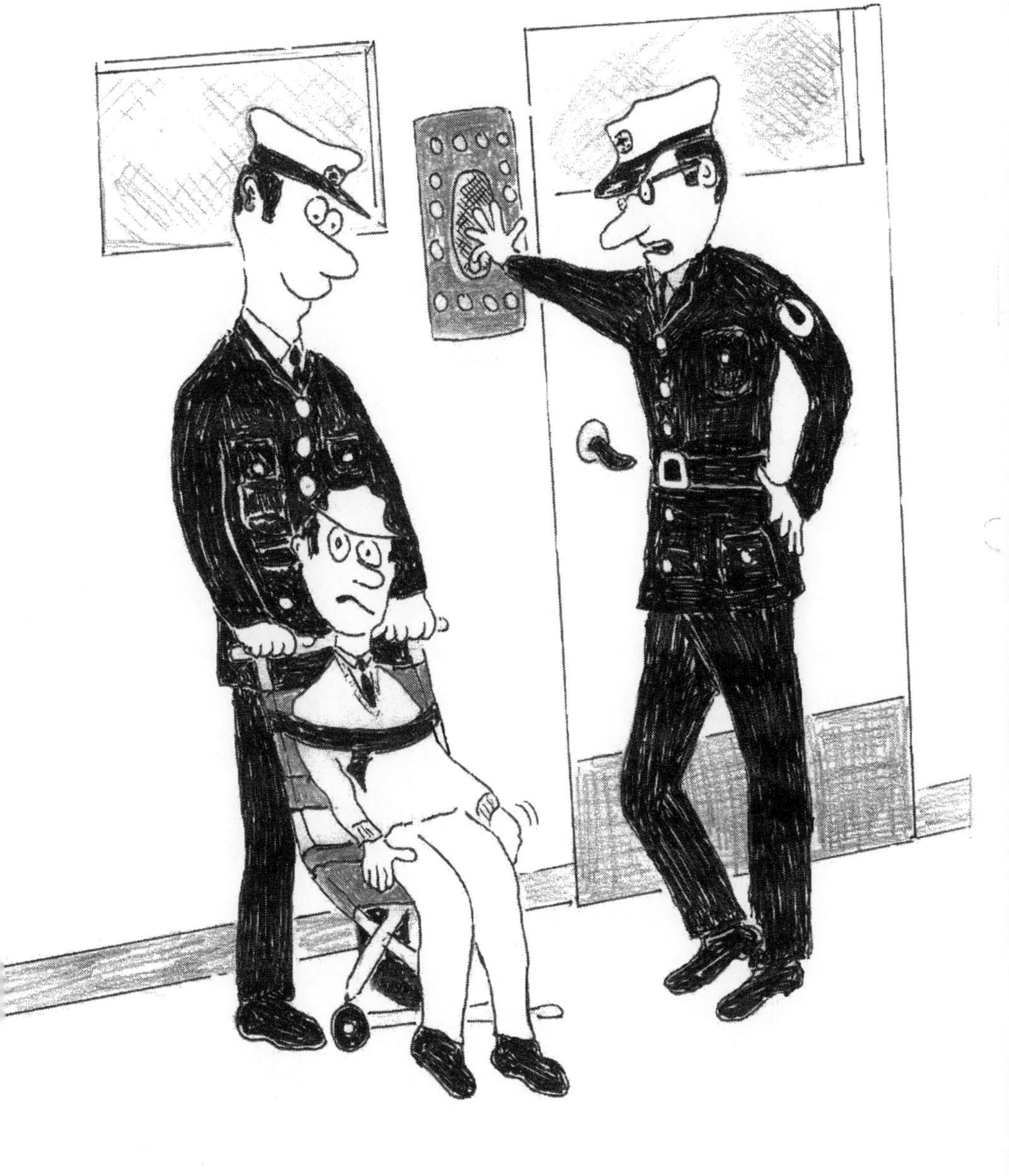

"Hope you've saved his tea luv?"

INSTANT RESPONSE

An emergency call to a night club on a Saturday night is not remarkable in itself. But when the crew are relying on local knowledge alone, things can go wrong.

The crew was told to attend to 'a male drunk with a head injury'. The crew members were confident that they knew where they were going, but on arrival they realised that they were at the wrong night club. However a drunk was on the phone there, ringing 999 and requesting an ambulance in slurred tones, because of a head injury. He was connected just as the ambulance arrived with its blue lights on.

The drunk slurred to the ambulance controller, 'You can forget it, the lads are already here'.

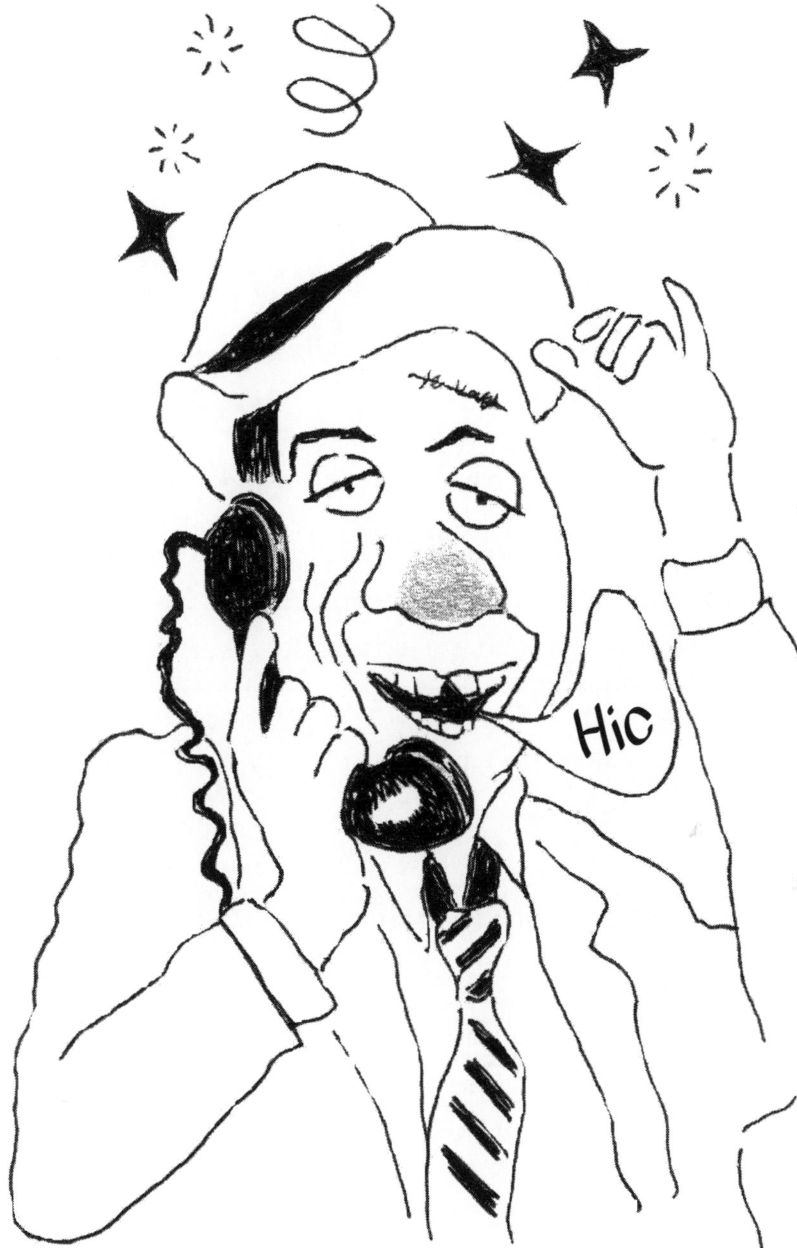
Hic

"Bloody fantastic service"!!!

YOU'RE A WIDOW, HAPPY NEW YEAR

A good bedside manner is undoubtedly, one of the greatest attributes of an ambulance man. As my old dad use to say, 'It's not what you say, but how you say it.'

Wise words, when at 23.45 hours on New Year's Eve a crew had the delicate task of breaking the sad news to a woman that her husband had passed away.

Any ambulance man will tell you that it doesn't matter how many years' experience you have, you can very rarely convey the right words when attempting to console a grieving relative. Just as they were preparing to break the news, the clock began to strike midnight.

The rookie ambulance man soon realised that wishing the grieving wife an enthusiastic 'Happy New Year' was not the best idea.

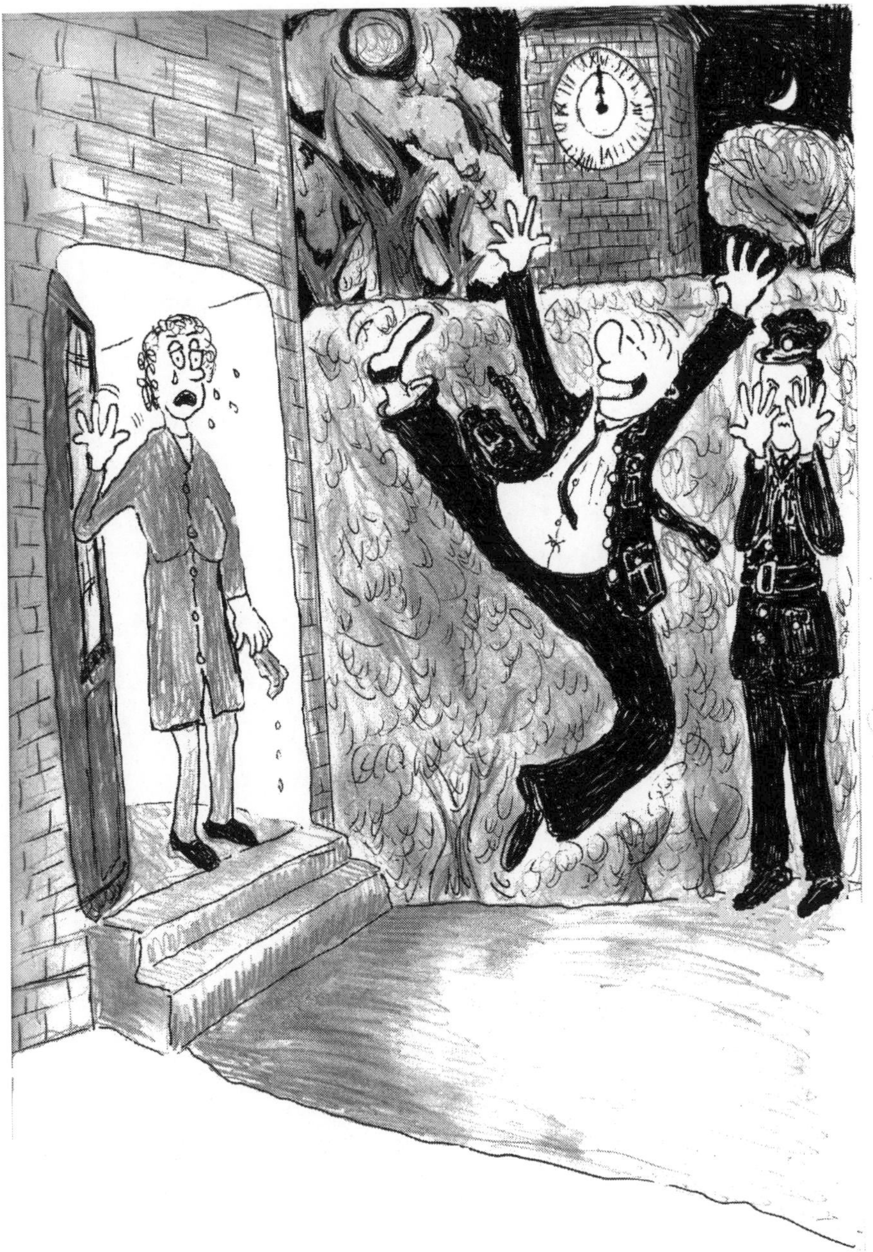

SEEN IT ALL BEFORE

The ambulance social club was always seen as a well-run organisation, especially when it was time for the Christmas party. At a meeting of the ambulance social committee, it was decided (by a narrow vote) to run an exclusive strip night at the local social club. This delighted the men, but their wives and girlfriends were outraged.

When the fateful night arrived, to the horror of the committee, the strip act was double booked. The girls never showed up. A crowd of over 50 ambulance men had paid over £1 a ticket for the event, so the quick-thinking committee went on a tour of the local red light district and hired a couple of raddled old prostitutes as replacements.

This was much to the disappointment of the guests, some of whom admitted having got to know the girls personally on their off days.

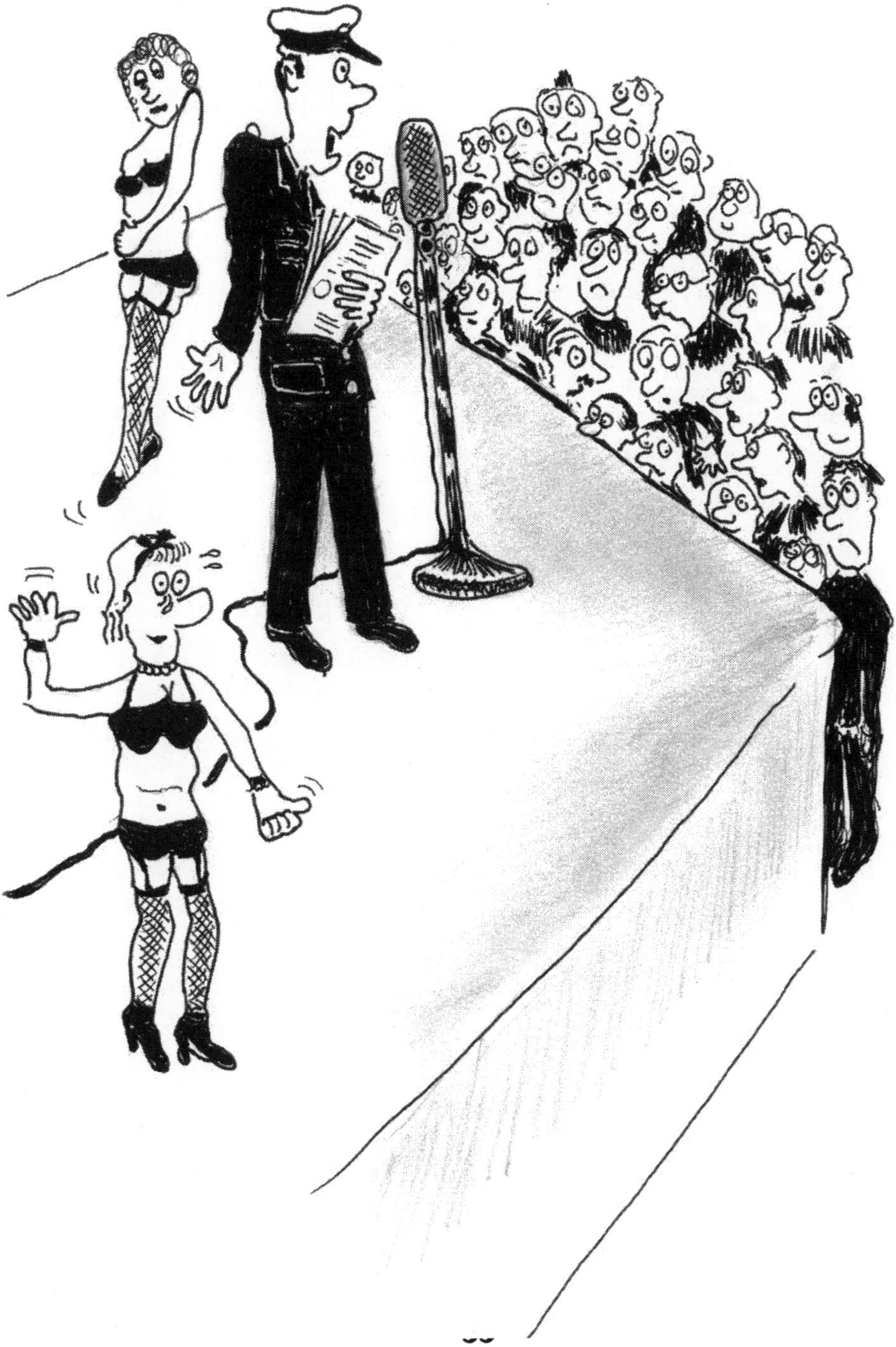

ONE SMALL STEP FOR MANKIND

A certain ambulance man's sense of humour was put to the test at a geriatric day unit. The crewman in question opened the back doors of his outpatient ambulance to allow his 'infirm patients' to board the vehicle.

His regular party trick was to purposely leave the folding rear steps in the up position, making the distance between the floor and the rear of the ambulance entrance approximately three feet in height, so it was impossible for the patient to step into the vehicle. 'Do you think you can manage that step?' he would say. The prospective passenger would quickly realise it was a joke and chuckle.

The exception to this rule was an 80-year-old lady, who took the question seriously. 'Yes, I think I can manage that' she said, and began to pull herself up by climbing the grab rail and wrapping her legs around the bottom of the adjacent holding bar.

After a quick puff on her inhaler she sat down ready for the journey home.

AMBULANCE
TRANSPORT

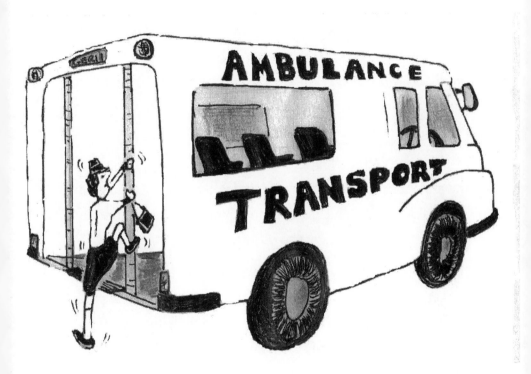

OWN GOAL

In the days when ambulances were not so busy it was considered acceptable to do the occasional quick 'foreigner' before the next call. Vic the ambulance man was desperate to pick up his repaired vacuum cleaner before the shop closed, and as it was only a half-mile round trip from the hospital to the repair shop and then home, the crew decided it was time to do the deed.

On completion of 'Operation Hoover' they started back towards hospital. As they hastily drove off they felt a bump on the side of the vehicle, but didn't think much about it and arrived back at the hospital in good time.

Control immediately assigned them a road traffic accident in the area they had just come from. On arrival at the scene they found a man lying in the road. He had been knocked off his push-bike by a passing ambulance…

The red-faced crew bandaged the patient's leg and sheepishly conveyed him to the hospital.

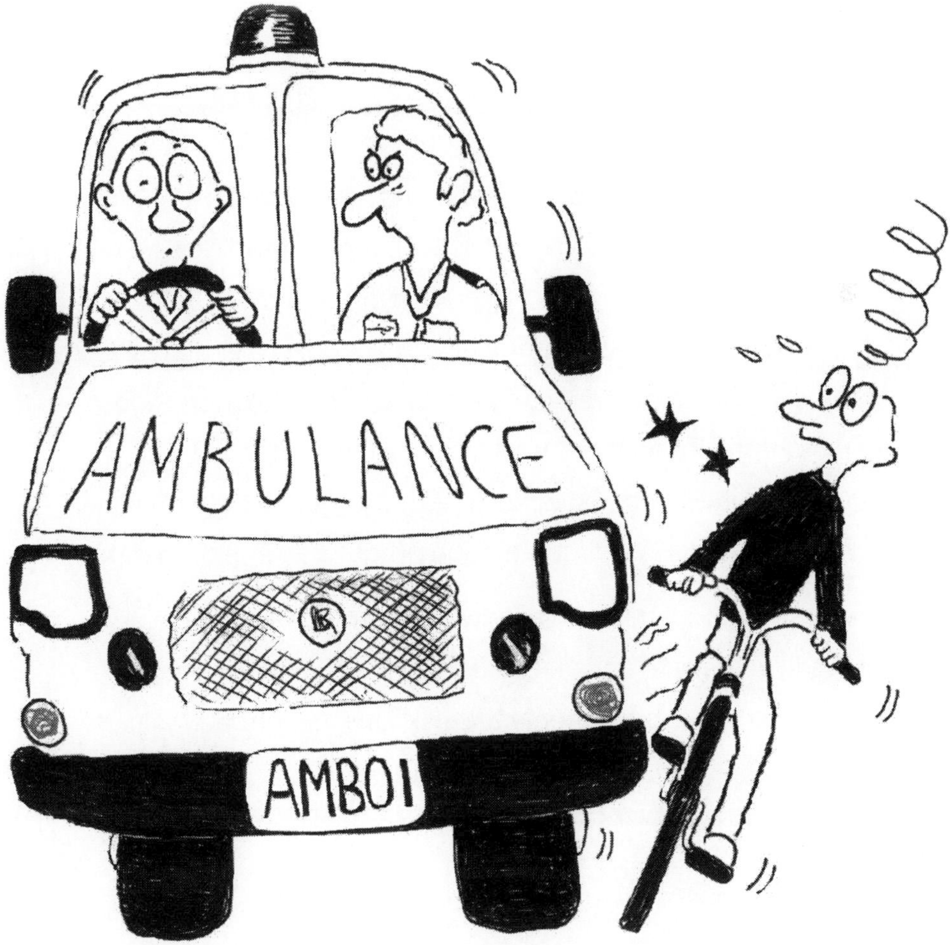
AMBULANCE
AMB01

DESPERATE FOR THE LOO

A major outbreak of food poisoning was discovered at a popular hotel in the centre of the city. The offending food was later discovered to be mayonnaise in the prawn cocktail. The consequences of approximately 100 people attending a company's dinner and dance award ceremony were horrendous. Frustration among the guests mounted regarding the lack of toilet facilities in the building. The guests needed the toilets very badly indeed, and the situation quickly became desperate,

In those days, all trauma cases went to a trauma hospital and all medical cases to another. A fleet of ambulances were called to transport not only the sick, but the injured.

The reason for so many injuries was the fighting to be next in line for the toilets.

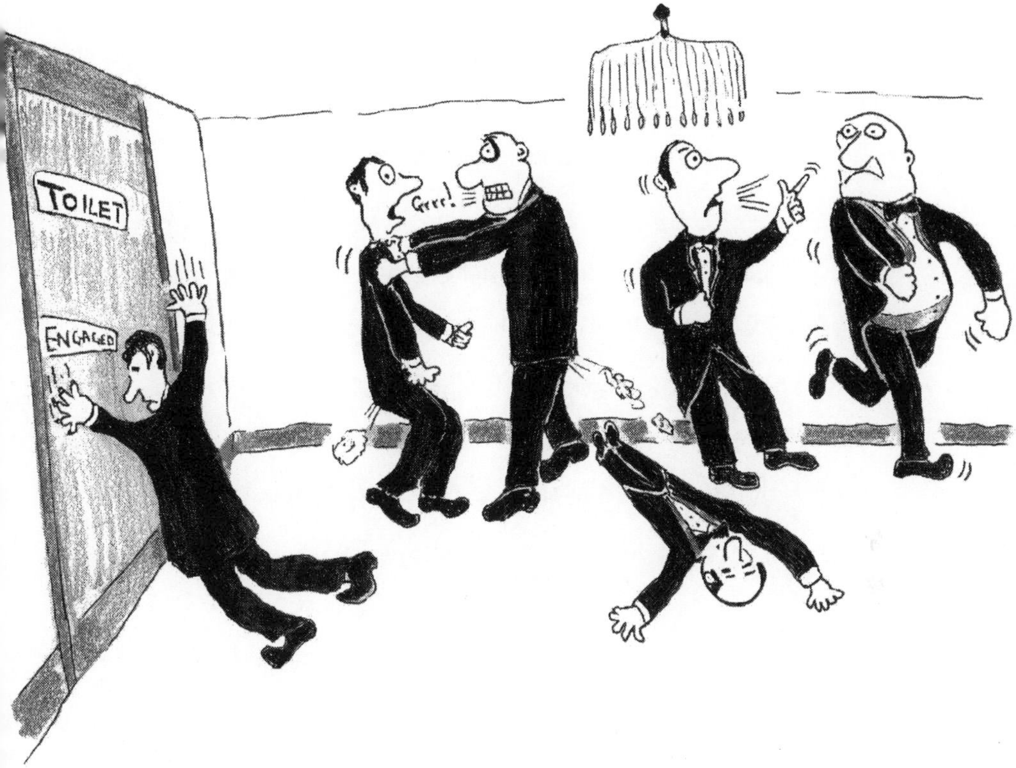
TOILET
ENGAGED
Grrr!

JUST POUR IT BACK IN, DEAR

A 999 call was passed to a night crew, who responded to reports of 'a worried lady bleeding from the leg'. On arrival, they had difficulty gaining access to the property.

The crew peered through the window to see an elderly female hobbling around, wearing a bucket on her right leg. They eventually attracted her attention and waited at the front door.

On first glance, they thought the lady had managed to trap her foot in the bucket, but further examination revealed that it was half full of blood, due to a ruptured varicose vein.

The crew sat the lady down, removed the bucket and raised both limbs. They continued to question the lady as to why her leg was in the bucket in the first place. 'I've kept all the blood' she said. 'Hopefully you will be able to pour it back into my leg and put a stitch in it, cos I can't go to hospital, I'm looking after my grandson in the morning.'

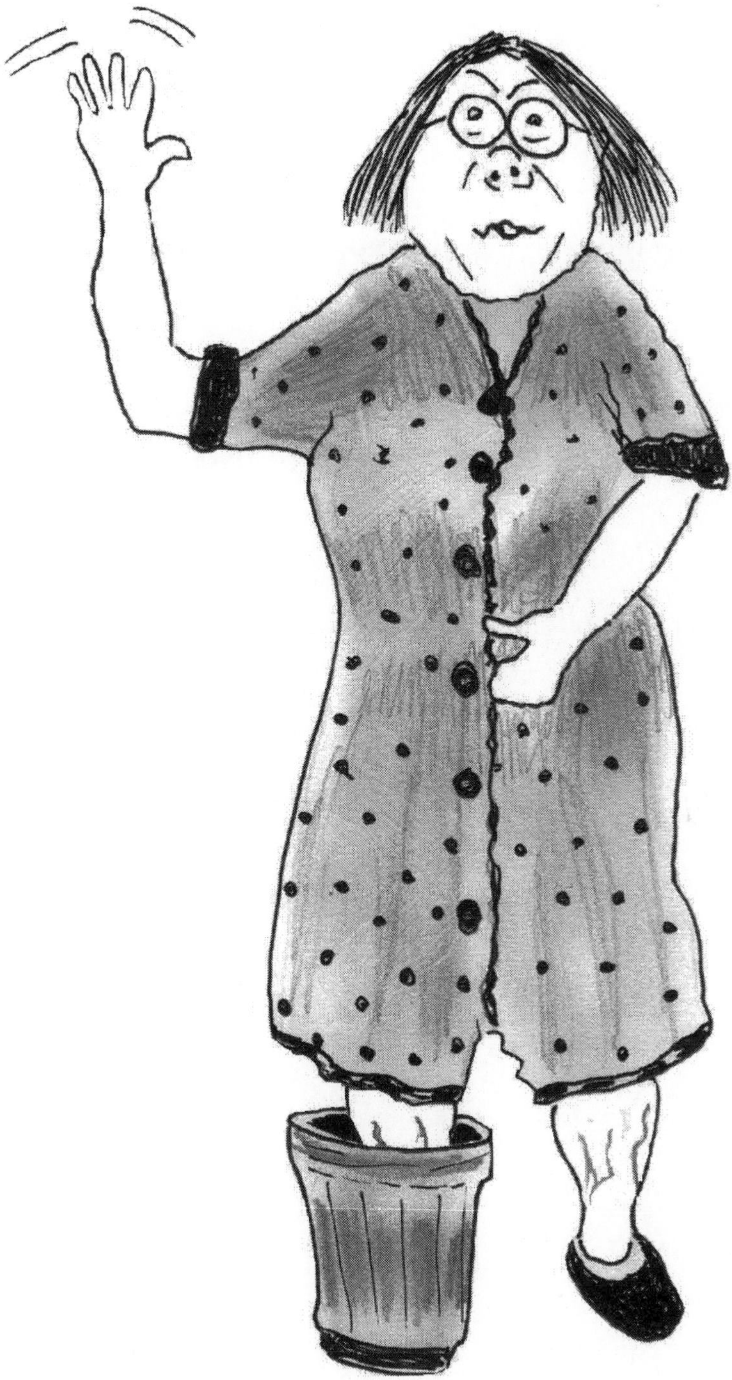

SNOW WHITE AND THE SIX DWARFS

A professional Christmas production of the pantomime *Snow White and the Seven Dwarfs* was about to be shown, and it was the final dress rehearsal before opening night. The producer was known by the cast for always trying to add a twist to the plot (within the script rules of course).

When fate took a hand and one of the dwarfs collapsed on stage, the ambulance was called. Unfortunately the crew were too late to help, as the poor man had passed away during the final scene.

One of the ambulance men who attended on that fateful night recalled watching as the patient was carted off stage by stretcher to hospital. To his alarm, both the producer and the MD were cheering.

"Bravo! What an exit!" they called out. They imagined that the cast had scripted a new ending to the show.

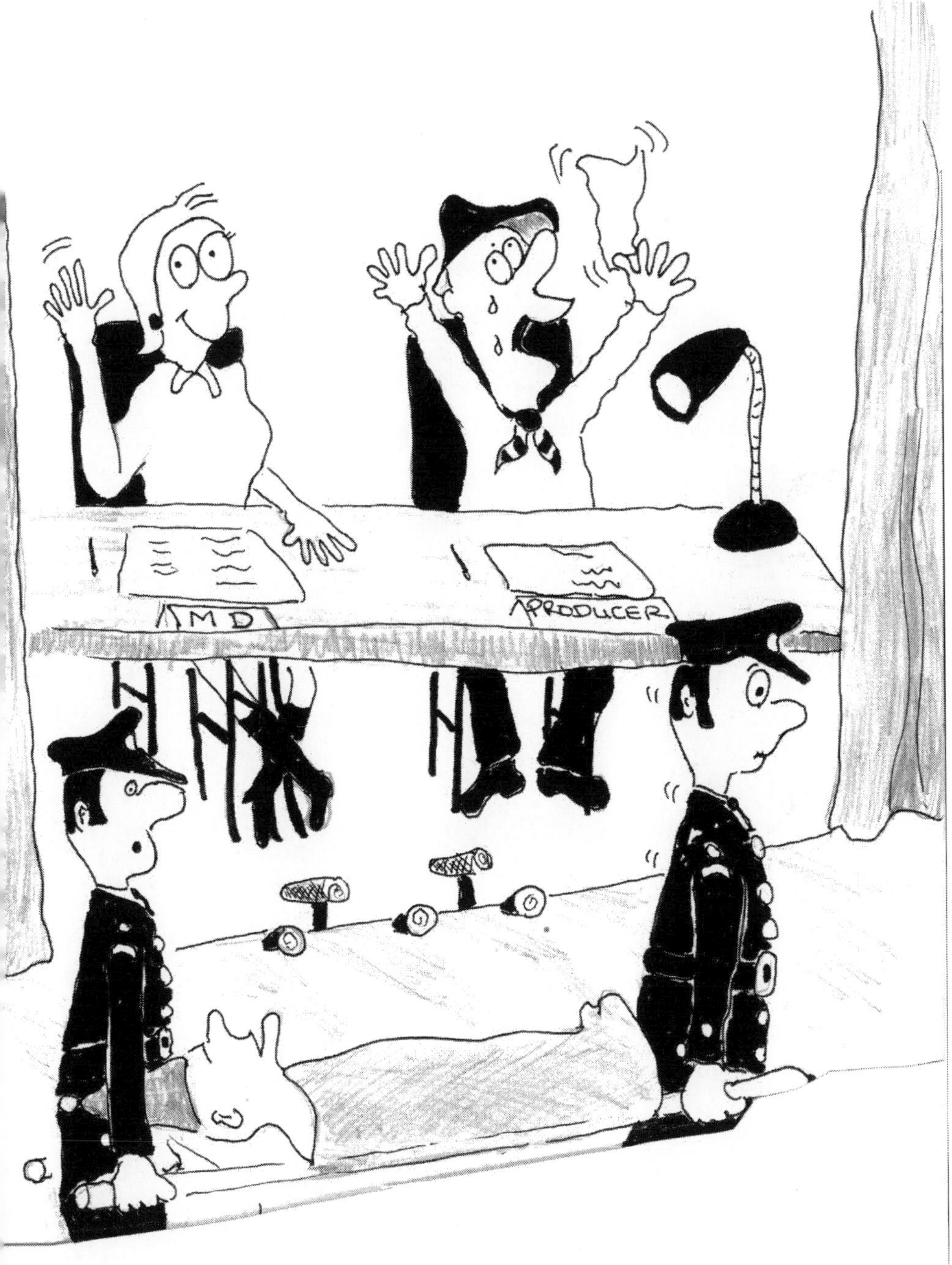
MD
PRODUCER

AN ARMLESS BIT OF CONFUSION

All three emergency services were called to a railway incident. First on the scene was the fire service, who found a man trapped between carriages, conscious, but with a severed arm. A policeman picked up the severed limb and placed it in his police car.

On arrival of the ambulance the firemen had managed to release the patient, but unknown to the police and ambulance services, the chief fire officer had asked for a medical team to attend the incident from the local casualty. Two doctors and three trained nursing staff were summoned at short notice. The policeman informed his control that he was on his way to casualty on blue lights with the severed limb.

The ambulance crew loaded the patient on to the stretcher and asked ambulance control to alert casualty. Just after the ambulance had departed, the medical team arrived at the railway station to be told the patient had already left.

First to arrive at casualty was the policeman with a severed arm but no patient, closely followed by the ambulance, with the patient minus his arm. Both emergency services were trying to hand over details to a student nurse, who was the only person left in casualty. Why? Because the medical team was attending a serious trauma incident on a railway track!

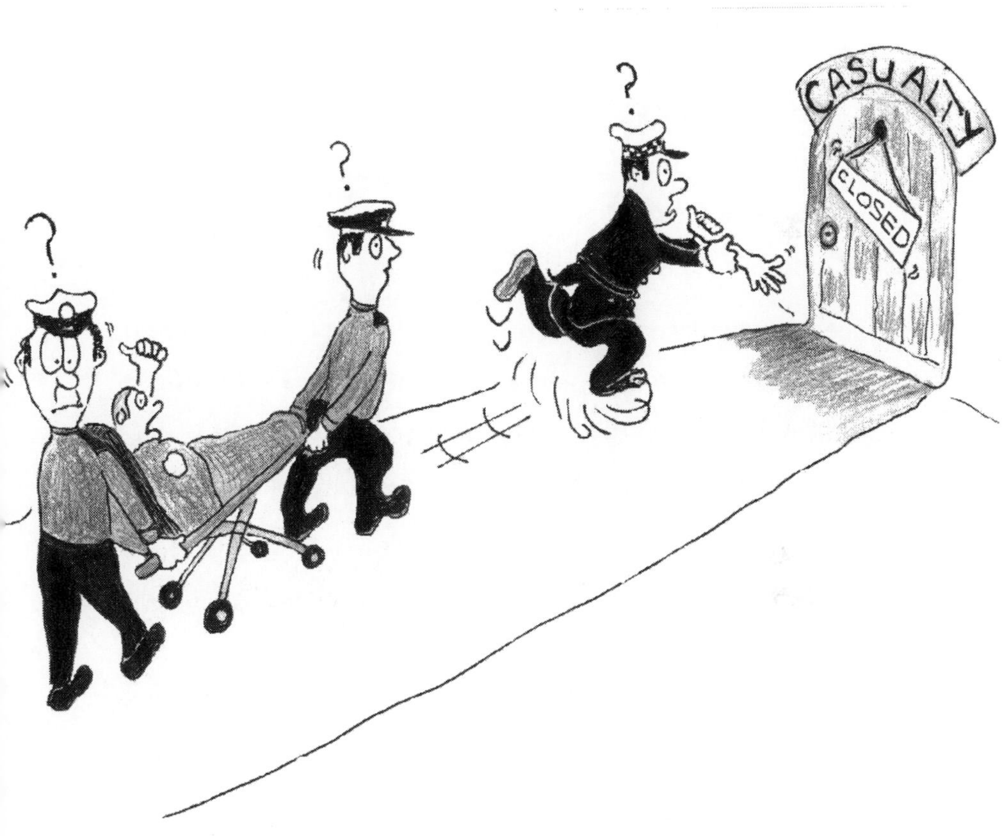
CASUALTY
CLOSED

THE WRONG HANDBAG

After an ambulance alert, casualty prepared to receive a 76-year-old woman in respiratory failure. A team of doctors and nurses were waiting in the resus department, but unfortunately, their attempts to sustain life were unsuccessful.

Procedure dictated that all the deceased's belongings had to be documented and placed in the hospital safe for the attention of the next of kin. Her only possession appeared to be a handbag which lay on the resus trolley.

The contents of the bag were checked by two nurses. They were shocked to find that it contained a can of Vimto, a yogurt, a large cheese sandwich, a contraceptive pill, a sanitary towel and an NHS pay slip. All was revealed when a worried student nurse working with the resus team declared that her handbag had gone missing.

SHAME TO WASTE IT...

A patient was taken into Accident & Emergency suffering from stomach pains. He was placed on a trolley and the ambulance man handed over the details of his findings to the nurses. He had purposely left the patient's belongings on the ambulance and on completion of his handover, he went back to the vehicle to gather the possessions.

Before returning, he emptied a tin of vegetable soup into a vomit bowl and went back into A & E with the patient's belongings and the bowl. He asked the nurses if they would require a sample of what was in the bowl. Both nurses quickly declined, so the ambulance man said 'Oh well, it would be a shame to waste the big bits' and started eating the contents, much to the horror of both nurses, who after witnessing what they had just seen, needed a vomit bowl themselves!

NARROW ESCAPE

When the ambulance crew arrived at a road accident, it was clear that a car had hit a bridge and slithered down the railway embankment. People were trapped inside the vehicle.

The attendant of the crew was often described as being as round as he was tall, and in his eagerness to get down the side embankment to attend to his patients, he unfortunately lost his footing. He carried on running and only came to a halt when he landed at the bottom - on the main London to Birmingham railway line.

His crewmate desperately attempted to radio control to ask for the trains to be stopped, but it was too late. As the London express raced down the track at 100 miles an hour, Mr Rotund somehow managed to clear the track and on an adrenaline rush, he ran up the embankment, shot into the ambulance and locked himself in the cab, suffering from shock.

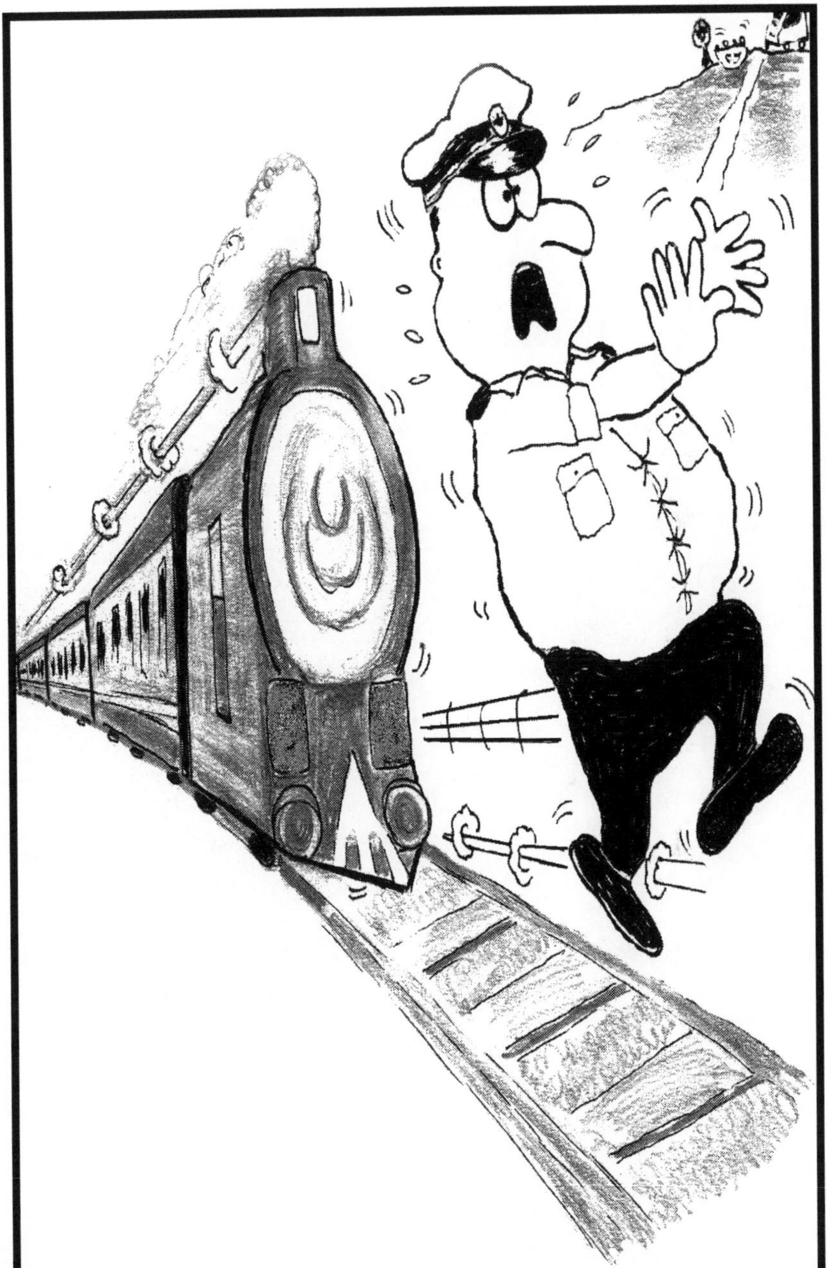

DOORS CLOSING...

The solo ambulance driver picked up eight patients from the outpatient department and was on his way to take them home, with the exception of one passenger who was to be escorted on to a train, leaving the railway station for London at 1500 hours. After putting on his flashing hazard warning lights, the ambulance man left his vehicle on the main road and slowly walked the patient on to the train.

Unfortunately, the train pulled out of the station with the unsuspecting ambulance man still on board. Not only was he trapped on a train for London, but he was answerable for abandoning seven passengers on an unmanned ambulance for four hours.

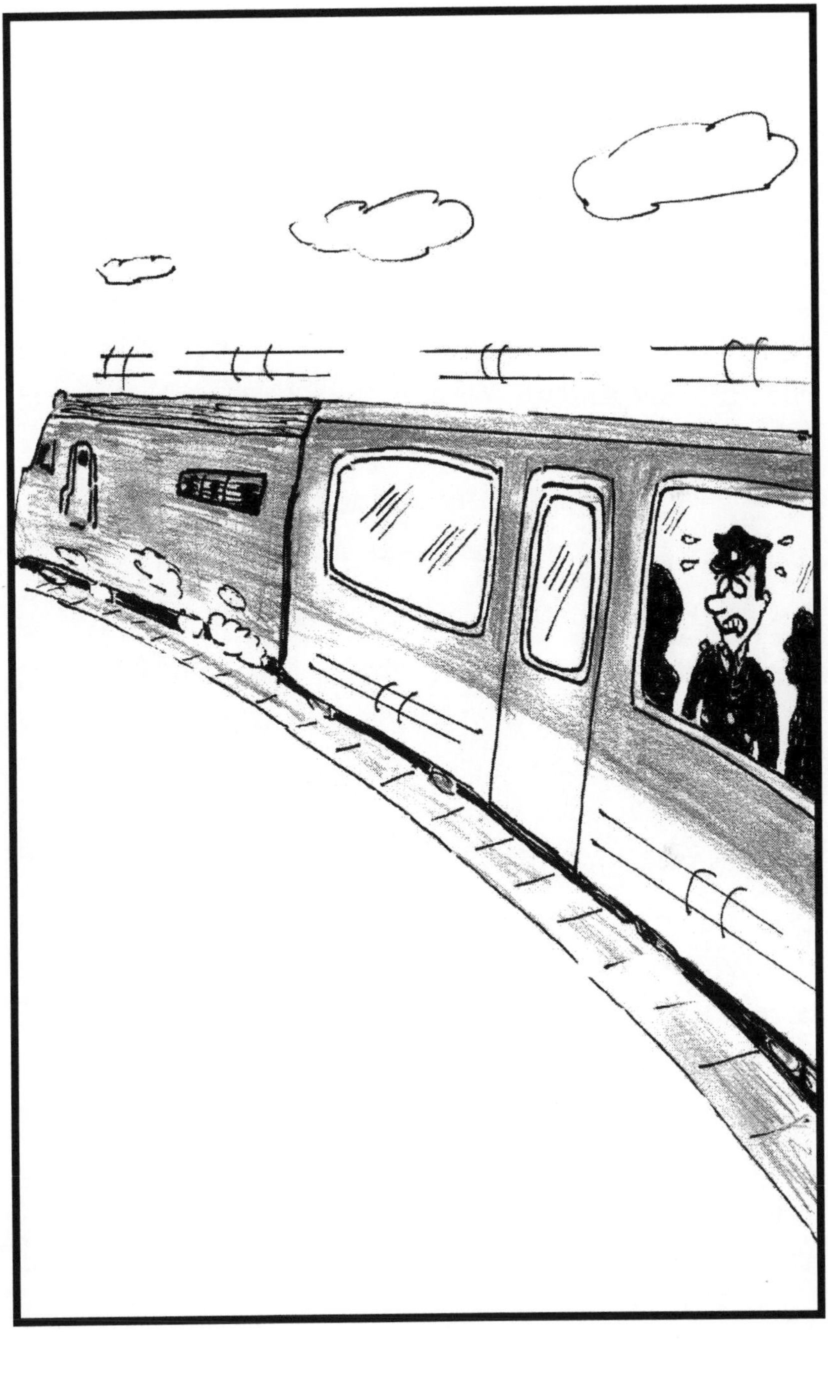

APPOINTMENT WITH DEATH

The following radio message was conveyed by ambulance control to an unsuspecting crew: 'Control calling ambo one, over.' 'Ambo one go ahead, over.' 'Thank you ambo one, we've had a call from a patient who's taken an overdose, he claims to be a trained assassin and wants to kill either a policeman or an ambulance man and as there are no police currently available, can you proceed with caution over?'

On arrival, the ambulance crew decided to approach the incident in Starsky and Hutch style, one crew member kicking the door open with his foot and his crewmate kneeling down and holding a torch as if he was posing with a gun. This procedure was repeated through all three doors, until the crew heard scuffling noises on entering the fourth and final door. As this last door was finally kicked open, nervous anticipation was at an all-time high and with hearts pounding, they both expected the worst.

What a let-down when they finally met the 'assassin', a 75-year-old stroke victim sitting in his wheel chair and harbouring an enormous grudge against the emergency services.

TECHNOSPEAK

By the beginning of the 1970s, ambulance training had improved to what was known as the Miller standard. A new training package required trainee ambulance staff to attend a six-week residential course, and although some of the training received has rarely been used in anger, at least trainees for the first time had formal theory and practical understanding.

Exams were introduced at the completion of each week, the students particularly enjoyed a first-aid crossword puzzle. The clues contained anatomical references and at the completion of the allocated time, the answers were read out by the instructor. To give an example, an eight-letter word meaning broken leg starting with FRA… answer, fracture.

However, not all minds thinks alike. When the question was asked 'What's the word for attempting to sustain life?' the first two letters were given as RE and the last four as TION. The instructor said, the answer was resuscitation, not f*****g reincarnation!

The same trainee was also asked what he would do in the case of intermittent claudication? (cramp). This bright spark said 'I would move the vehicle 100 yards down the road and radio control again'.

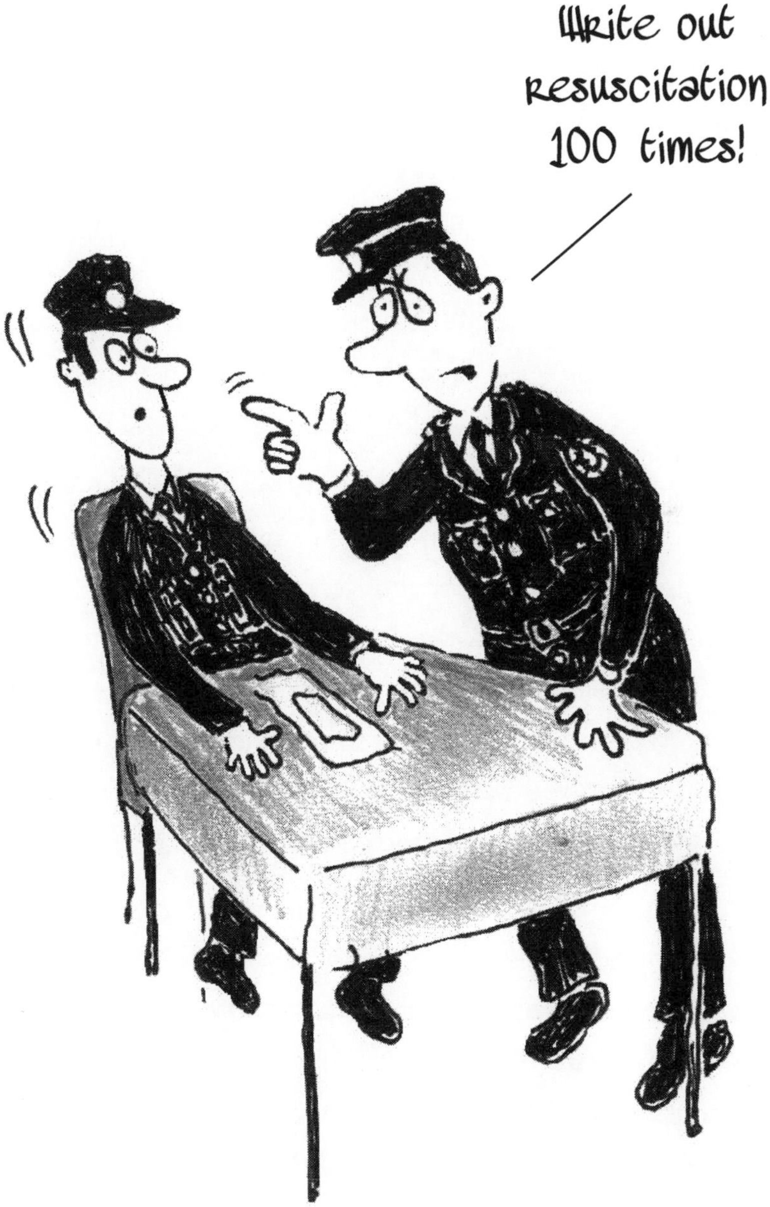
Write out resuscitation 100 times!

WALKIES!

One of the crew members had only recently joined the ambulance service after being honourably discharged from the RAF as a dog handler. When approaching the scene of an RTA, the crew could see a car on its roof with a person trapped behind the wheel.

On arrival, one of the crew went directly to the injured person and supported the neck and spine in anticipation of his crewmate bringing a stretcher and a cervical collar. The ex-RAF man unfortunately had other ideas. Still in dog handling mode, he snatched a dog off the attending police officer and assumed his previous RAF role of haring off across the field to look for clues to the accident, leaving his crewmate holding the head and neck of the entrapped patient.

The attending ambulance man embarrassingly had to ask the police to dial 999 to request a second crew, as he couldn't let go of the patient's head and neck due to further possible injury. When the backup crew arrived, they asked the ambulance man, where his colleague was. He replied 'He's running across the field with a police dog sniffing for evidence of the crash'!

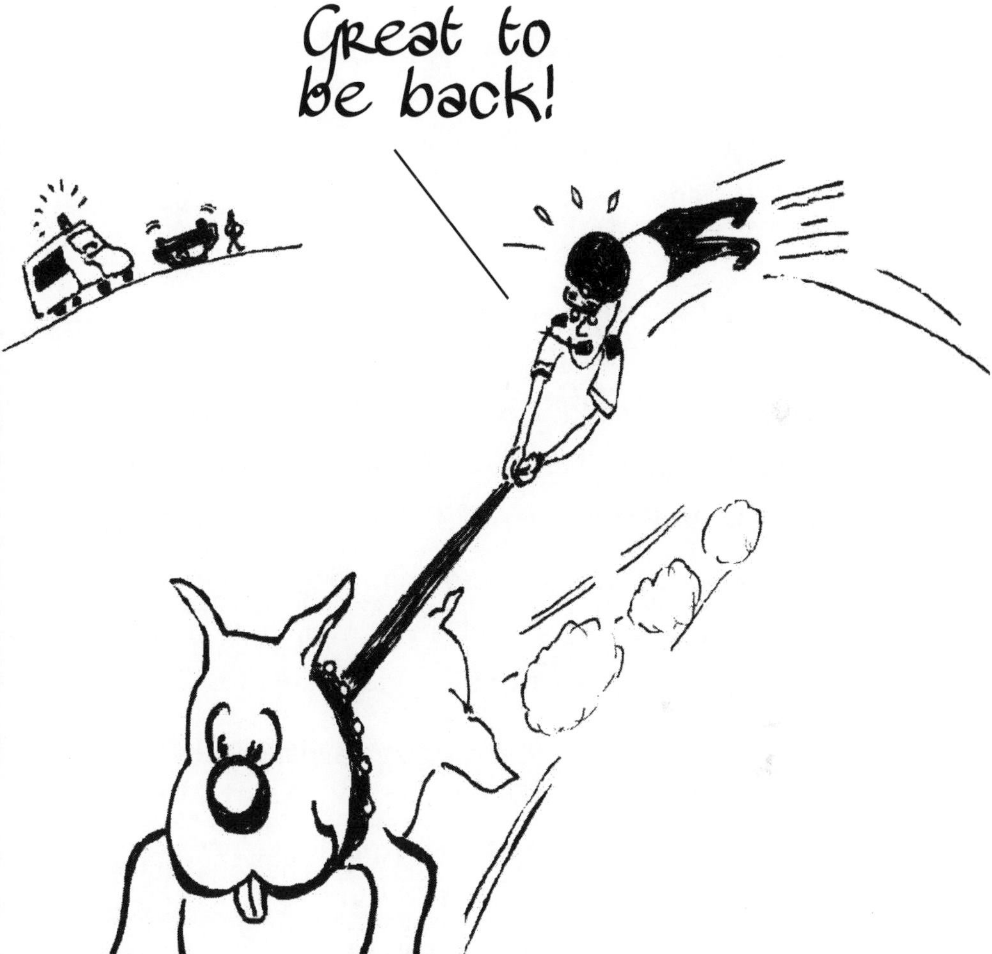
Great to be back!

LOST ON THE A45

In the 1970s there were no such things as sat nav or tracking systems. Ambulance crews had to rely on road maps and local knowledge alone.

A crew was asked by emergency control to go and find a recently-recruited outpatient driver who had got lost after picking up his patient from a local hospital for discharge. The emergency ambulance crew was told the rookie outpatient driver was lost somewhere on the A45 south of Rugby.

The crew asked control if they knew how long the A45 was. Control replied 'Yes, but the ambulance driver doesn't know where he is and the patient isn't quite sure either.'

The next question asked by the crew was where had the patient been discharged from. The reply came back 'Hawthorne Ward'. This was a psycho-geriatric dementia unit, and the rookie PTS driver had been driving for an hour and a half under the patient's instructions.

The emergency ambulance eventually found the PTS ambulance some way past Northampton, 25 miles from the patient's home.

AMBULANCE
AM
LEFT RIGHT!
LEFT RIGHT!
OUT PATIENTS

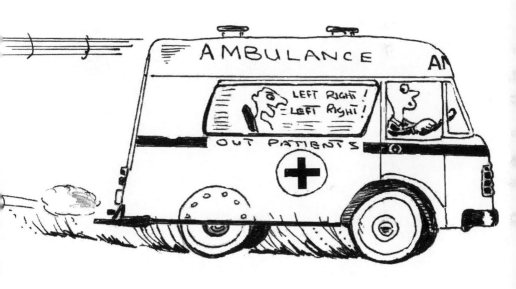

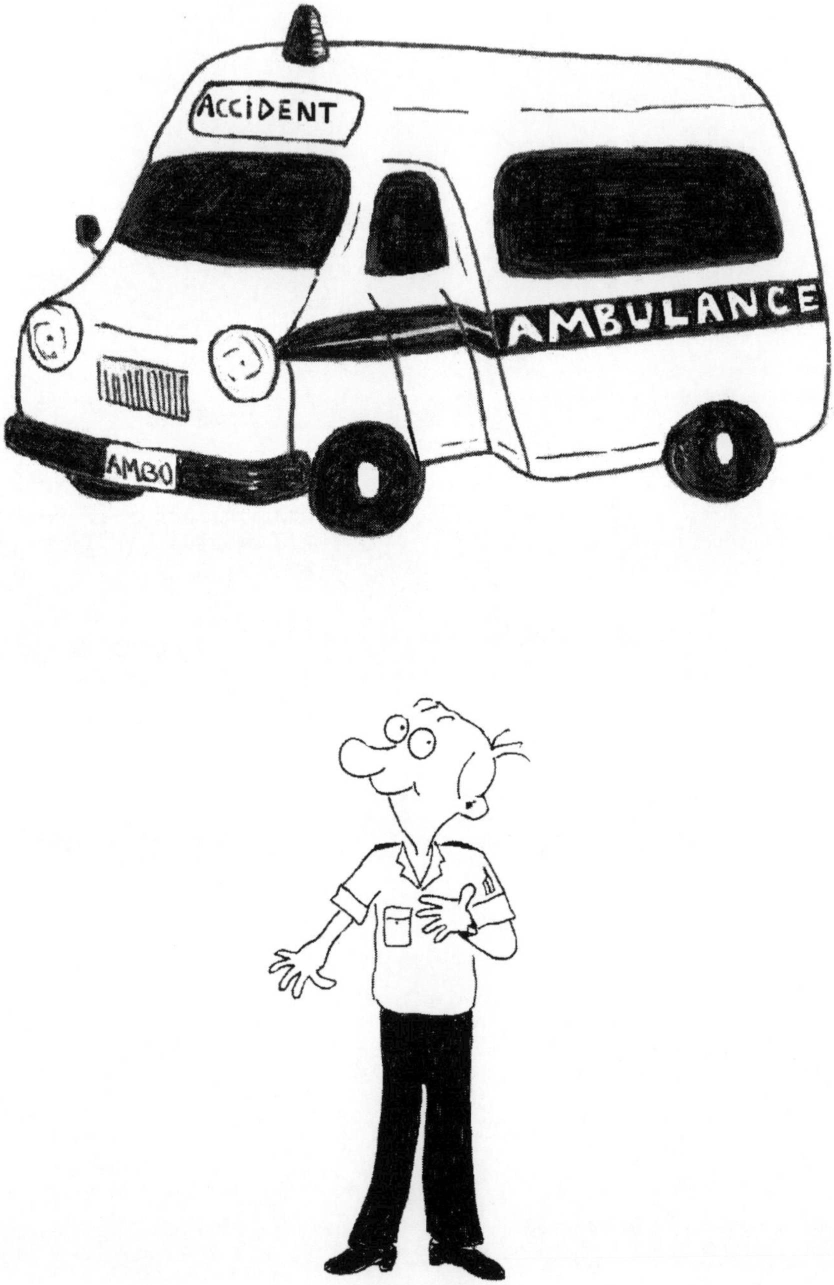
ACCIDENT
AMBULANCE
AMBO

THE 1980'S

WOODEN OVERCOAT

UNINTENDED MEANINGS

TERROR ON THE 4.55

NOT JUST A KISS OF LIFE...

NOT KNOWN AT THIS ADDRESS

CAT SCAN

HAPPINESS IS A WARM STRETCHER

BACK-SEAT DELIVERY

I'M NOT DEAD, HONEST

ANYTHING YOU CAN DO, I CAN DO BETTER

KEEPING ABREAST OF VITAL SIGNS

FINAL VOYAGE

WHAT A WAY TO GO

WARM RESPONSE FROM THE PUBLIC

THE BUNGLING SUICIDE

FREE SUN ROOF CONVERSION

HOW TO LOSE SEVEN PATIENTS

SHE ADDER NASTY SHOCK...

THE RIGHT SIGNATURE TUNE

OUT OF THE FRYING PAN...

WOODEN OVERCOAT

An ambulance man had the misfortune to suffer a chest pain while on duty. He was admitted to hospital and placed on a heart monitor as a precaution while the necessary blood tests were taken to reveal the cause of the problem.

His so-called shift mates were constantly playing tricks on each other, and when they were given a hospital transfer to the same ward as their poorly shift mate, and saw him lying in his bed asleep, the crew decided to make a random visit to see him.

They soon realised that the casualty sister did not think it was at all funny that they had taken a tape measure to measure their colleague up for a box.

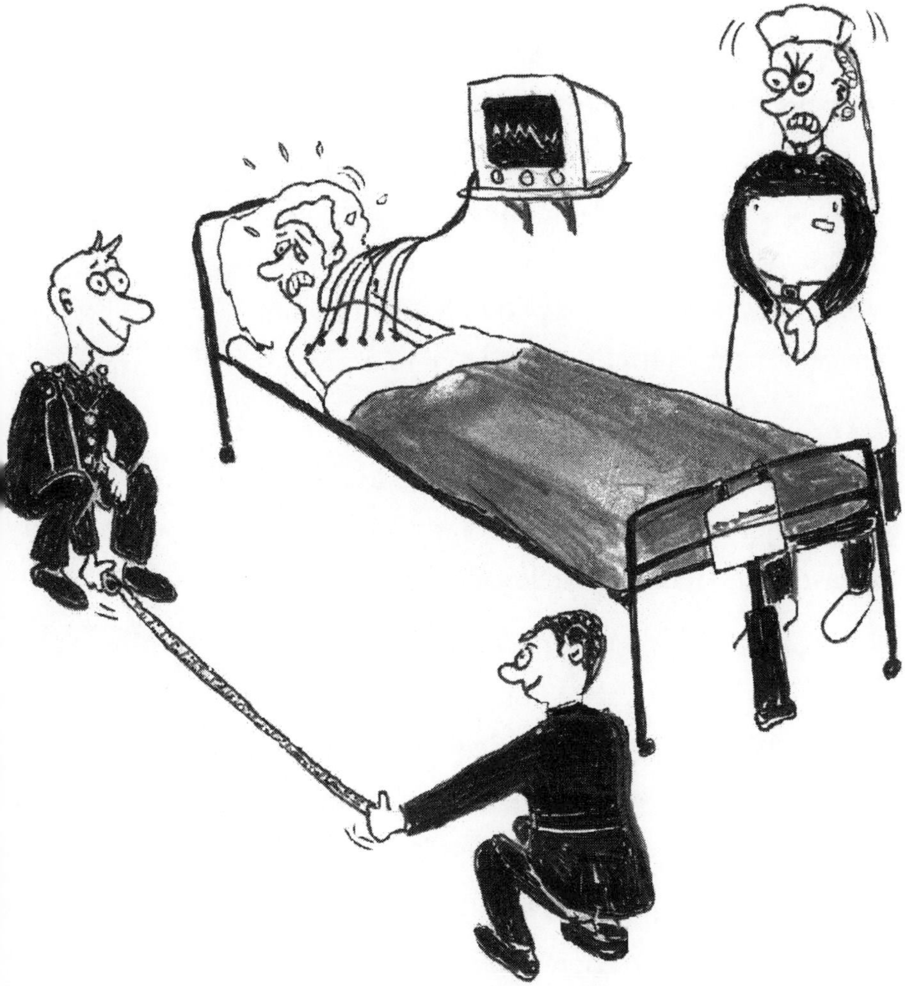

UNINTENDED MEANINGS

In the 1980s one of the first responder cars came into operation to supplement the conventional ambulances, and the word 'paramedic' (or extended trained ambulance staff) started to be introduced into the service. In a naive attempt to operationally introduce this new breed of ambulance person, it was suggested that teams of two or three paramedics could team up in a car with a driver and roam the area, responding to paramedic calls.

The plan was eventually abandoned as poorly thought through, not least the name. No one noticed what the initials of 'Fast Action Response Team' spelled out until the vehicles had been liveried up.

The service was keen to promote the words 'paramedic unit' on the side sliding doors of a new fleet of vehicles. But the livery had to be altered yet again, because when the side door slid backwards the letters 'PARAMED' were lost, advertising 'DIC UNIT'.

On top of this, both vehicle number plates incorporated the letters DOA, an abbreviation for 'dead on arrival.'

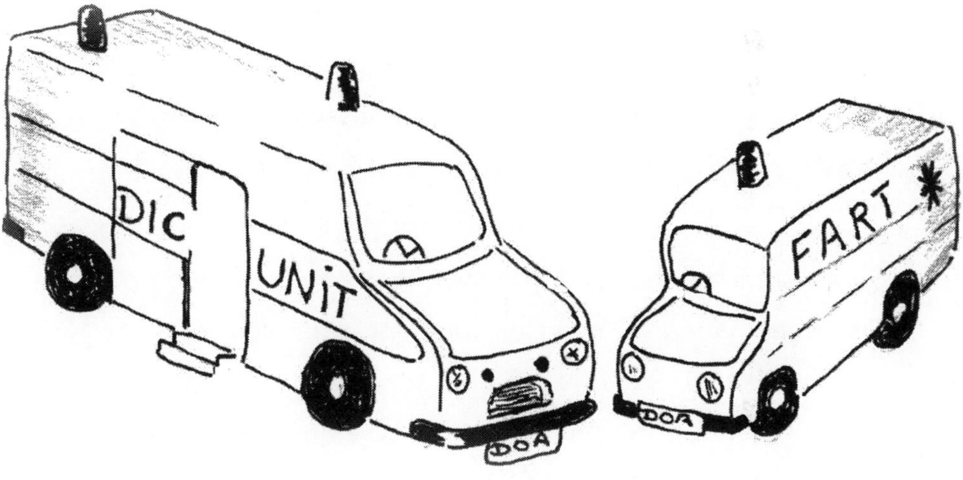
DIC
UNIT
DOA
FART
DOA

TERROR ON THE 4.55

The ambulance service is a diverse organisation, with multiple disciplines and skills to its bow. One part of the organisation involves planning exercises in preparation for major incidents. Such was the case on a train one day, where the Emergency Planning Officer was planning an exercise and confirming the details on his mobile phone to ambulance headquarters. Unfortunately the officer was not wearing uniform and passengers did not know who he was as they listened to the following one-sided conversation:

'So, it's Birmingham Airport, in daylight on the 4th involving a passenger plane?... 90 dead, do you think it should be more?... OK make it 95. 35 serious injuries sounds about right. 70 walking wounded? No problem, should be manageable. Good work, we will all meet at 1400 hours to plan the final details.'

The passengers were not only frightened but outraged. How could a terrorist talk in public so flippantly about a forthcoming attack? A message was conveyed via the on-board ticket inspector to Birmingham Railway Police, who had some questions to ask the 'Birmingham One'.

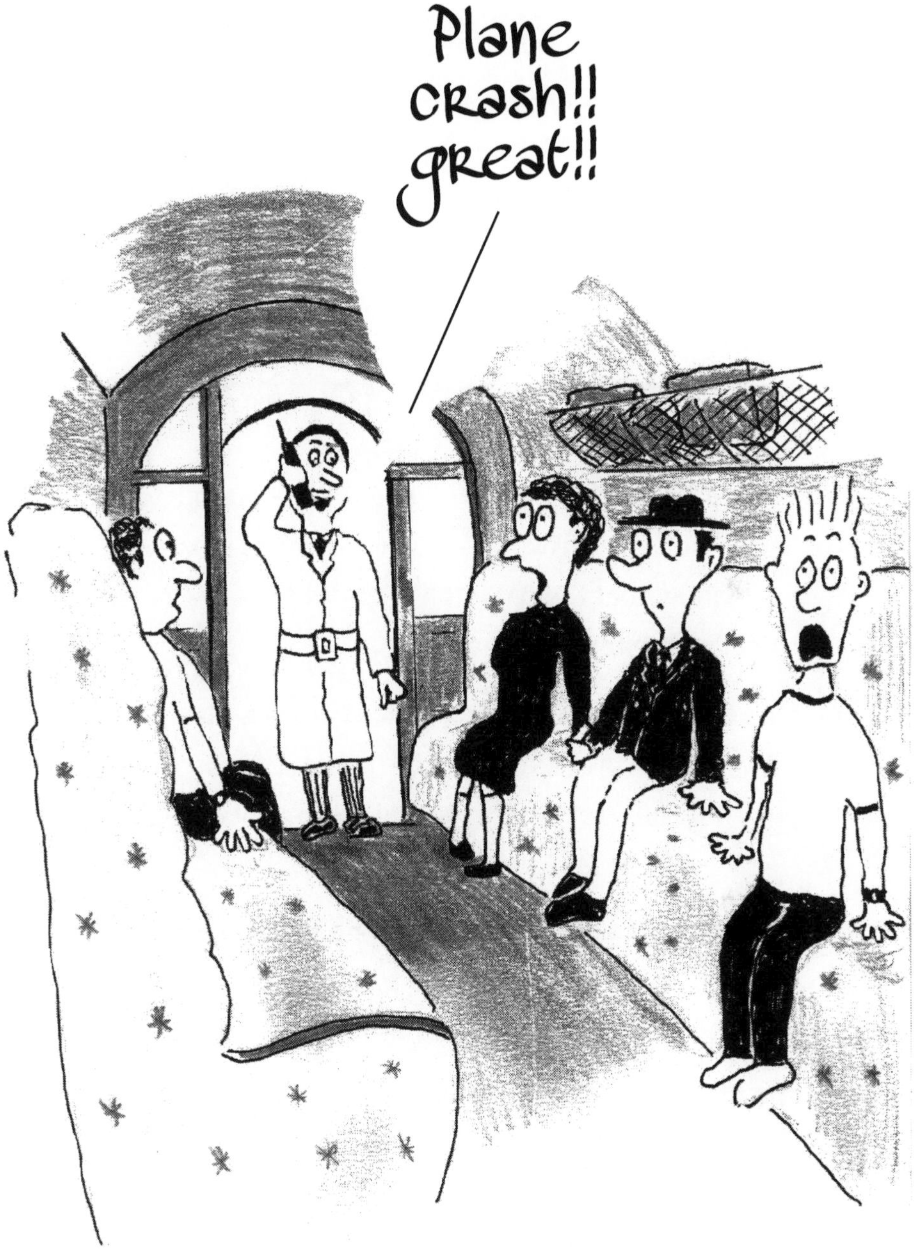
Plane crash!! great!!

NOT JUST A KISS OF LIFE...

An ambulance was called to an 80-year-old female alcoholic who was drunk. On arrival the crew was met by her family, who explained that the patient was bed-ridden and even called the taxi to go and collect her alcohol.

Her family were showing obvious signs of distress in what was more of a social problem than an ambulance case. The ambulance man felt sorry for the family and decided to go and talk to the old lady.

But before he could get a word in, the little old lady instructed him to climb into bed and make mad passionate love to her, to the acute embarrassment of all.

For the first time this ambulance man was lost for words.

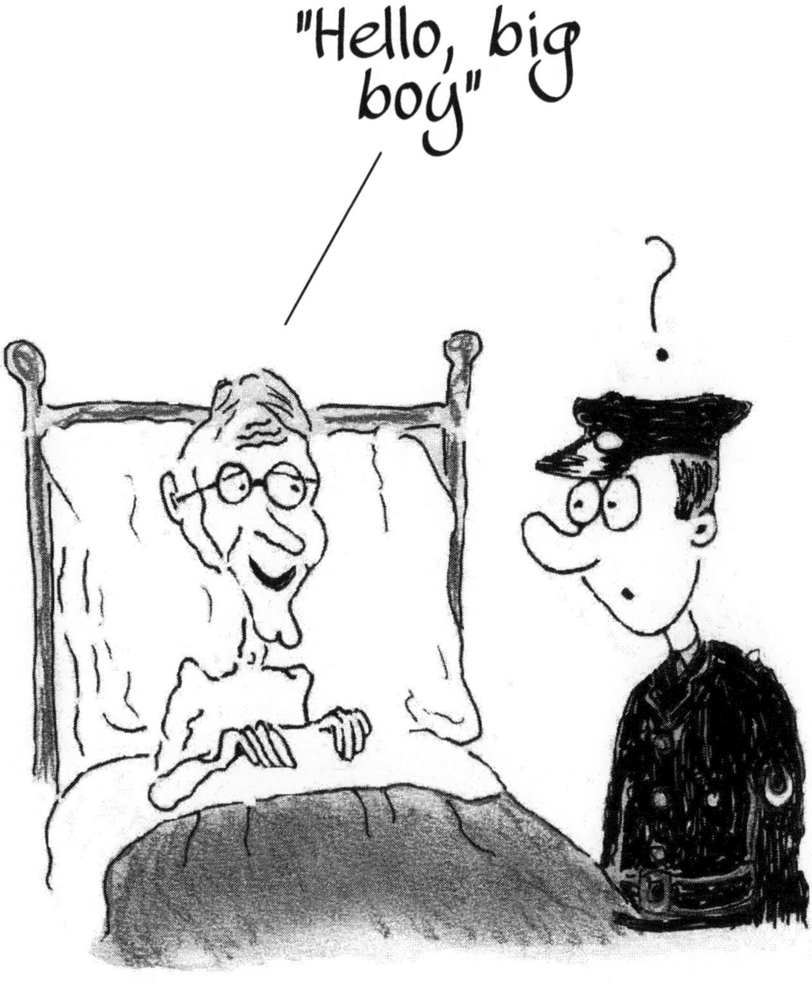
"Hello, big boy"
?

NOT KNOWN AT THIS ADDRESS

Andy and John were an ambulance discharge crew who had been given six patients to drop off. The last of the six was Joan, of number 5 Red Lane. On arrival at Joan's address, Andy saw a gentleman tending to his garden and shouted to him, 'have you got a wheelchair for the patient, mate?' He replied 'No I'm sorry I haven't', to which Andy replied 'It's OK, we'll use ours.'

Joan was wheeled in on the carry chair into the front room and placed on a comfy chair. When the crew came out, the chap in the garden said 'What are you going to do now?' Andy replied 'We've finished for the day, we've put Joan in your front room.' The man replied 'She doesn't live here. She's nothing to do with me!'

The crew had no choice but to take her back to hospital, only to discover that poor Joan had senile dementia. Although she had once lived at number 5 Red Lane, she had moved away 20 years ago.

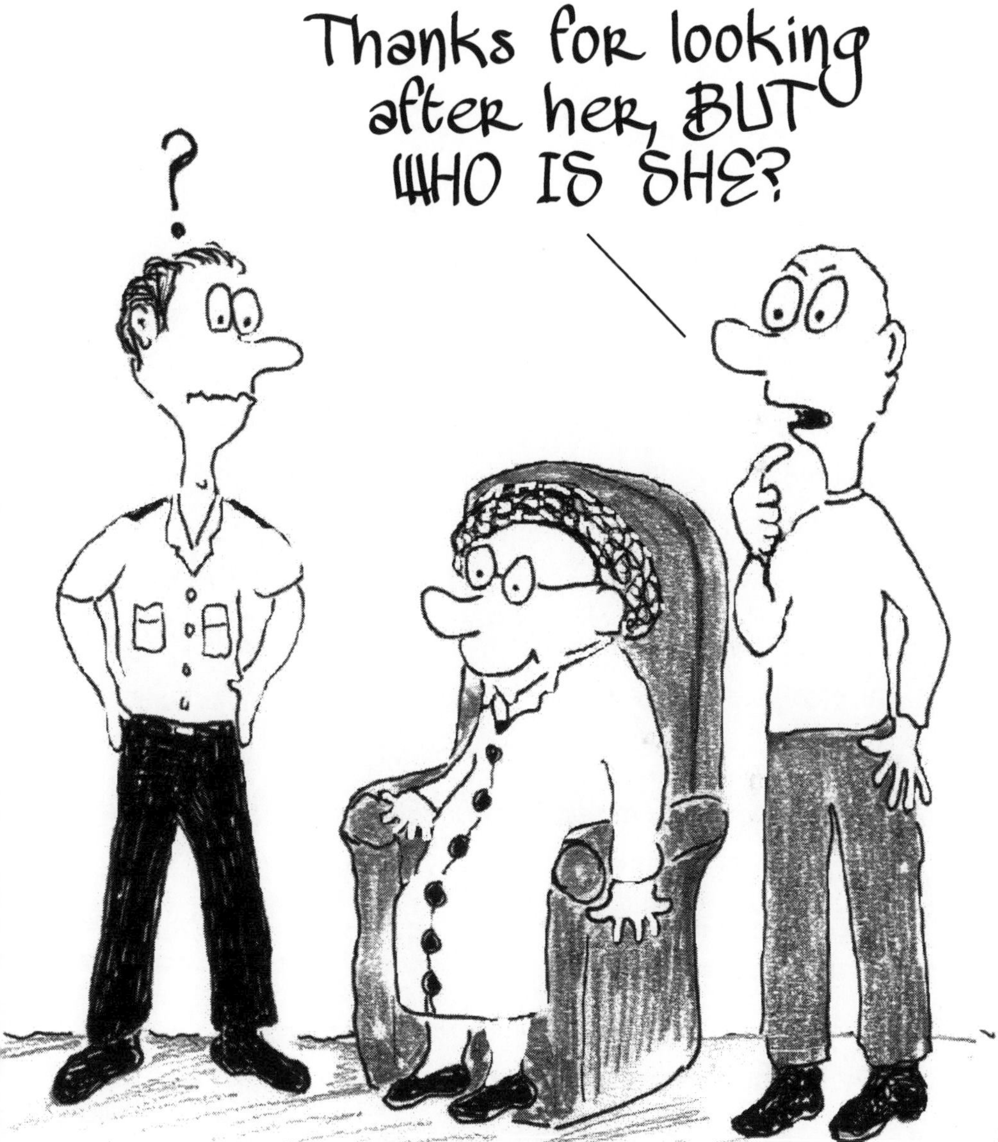
Thanks for looking after her, BUT WHO IS SHE?
?

CAT SCAN

Police were called by a neighbour to a house disturbance. On arrival they found a female unconscious on the floor, with traces of blood on her clothes. Police were querying attempted murder as the ambulance arrived.

The crew assumed the patient had been lying on the floor for some time, as she was very cold. Information gathered revealed that the patient was an insulin-dependent diabetic. The crew thought she might be in a diabetic coma.

The patient was about to be wheeled out of the house and taken off to hospital when a loud clattering noise was heard coming from the kitchen.

The neighbour who raised the alarm, shouted, 'That's it! That's the disturbing noise I've been hearing.'

Police, ambulance crew and the neighbour all peered around the door into the kitchen, where they discovered the owner's bloody and half-starved cat with a tin of cat food welded to its head, banging the tin desperately on a radiator in a vain attempt to loosen it!

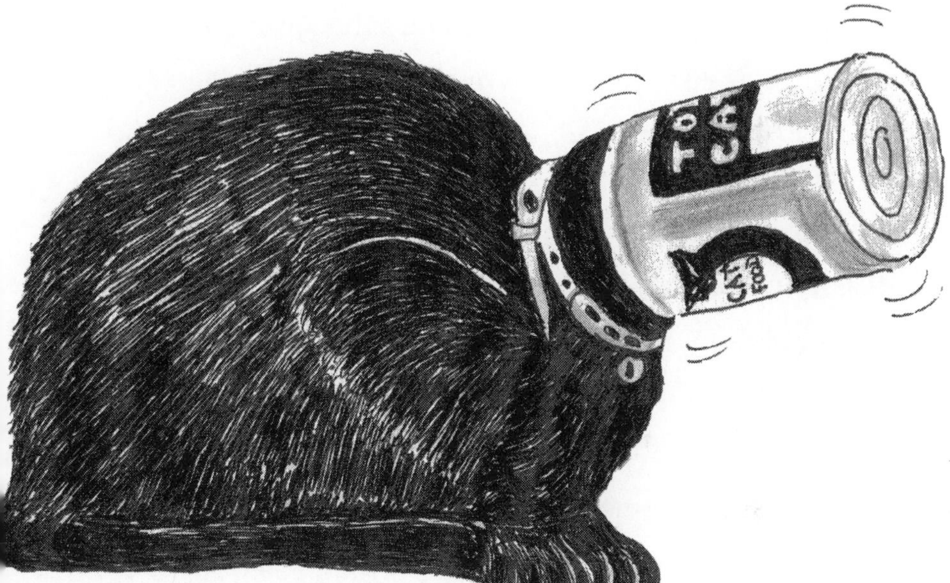
CAT
FOOD

HAPPINESS IS A
WARM STRETCHER

On a night shift, a good three hours of 'rest' had gone by before the next shout, when the ambulance driver, was called to attend a maternity case. His mate was lying sound asleep on the stretcher of the ambulance, and although the driver shouted to wake his mate, it was having little effect. The situation became rather embarrassing as the crew approached the patient's address with the mate still asleep on the stretcher.

The ambulance driver stopped the vehicle 200 yards short of their destination, opened the ambulance doors and shook his mate until sleepy head slurred the words, 'All right, I'm awake!' The driver continued slowly to give his mate a little time to get his uniform on.

As the ambulance turned into the patient's street, both patient and mum were waiting outside the house. 'Sleepy head', meanwhile, had just managed to get off the stretcher, stand up and put his shirt and trousers on as the back doors of the ambulance opened and the expectant mum boarded the vehicle, immediately lying on the stretcher the dozing mate had just vacated.

There was a smile of delight on the expectant mother's face as she turned to her mum and said, 'Ooh Mum, it's a modern-day miracle, this stretcher's heated!'

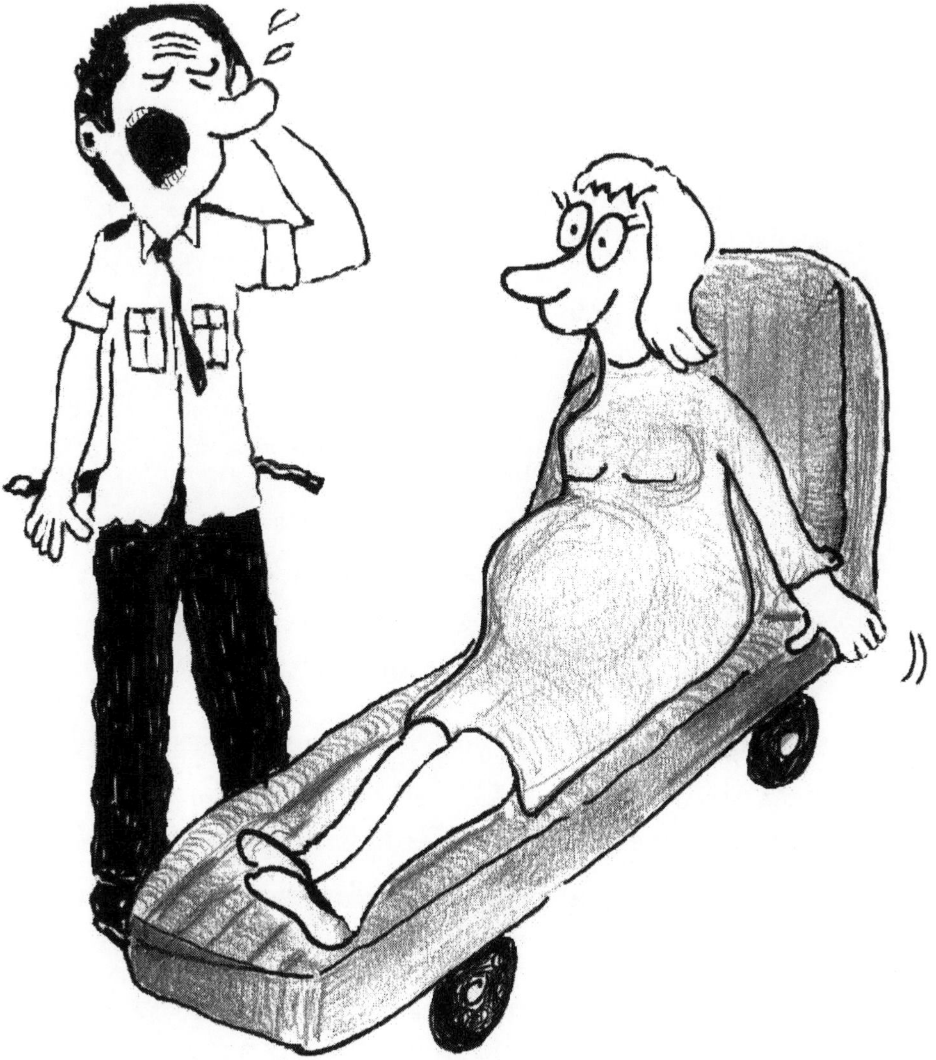

BACK-SEAT DELIVERY

The birth of the baby was imminent, and on arrival of the crew the expectant mum decided to stretch out as well as she could in the back of her car by pushing the front seats forward. One of the crew members gave her Entonox analgesic (gas and air) as his colleague climbed into the rear of the vehicle in readiness for the pending birth.

At first, the expectant mum was very nervous and anxious regarding the forthcoming event, but once the Entonox started to work its magic it made her feel a little more relaxed - to such a degree that in between the labour pains she started to giggle nervously.

The crew was trying to be as professional as possible in a very embarrassing situation, but this made the expectant mum giggle even more between contractions. The crew member who was about to deliver the baby asked her whatever she was finding to laugh about.

She replied 'The last time I was in the back seat of this car in this position with a man between my legs, I conceived this baby!'

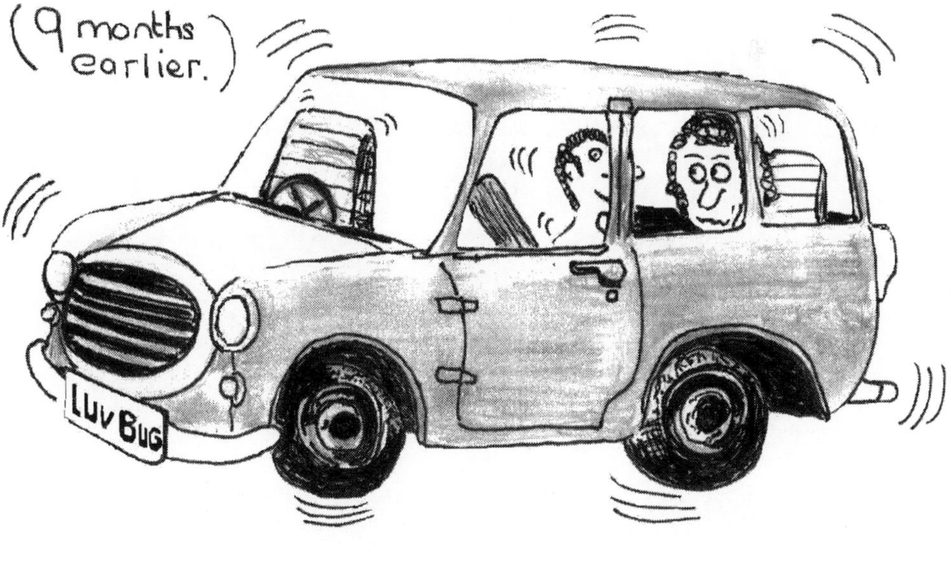
(9 months earlier.)
LUV BUG

I'M NOT DEAD, HONEST

As the long serving ambulance technician entered the dimly-lit house, he was led to a male patient collapsed on the floor. The patient was extremely pale and there was blood oozing from his nose.

The technician had always prided himself on certifying death without using any of this 'modern equipment nonsense', and on a quick examination he declared to the relatives that their loved one was deceased. The patient immediately opened his eyes and said 'No I'm not.'

It certainly wasn't the response the technician had expected, but there didn't seem much point in arguing.

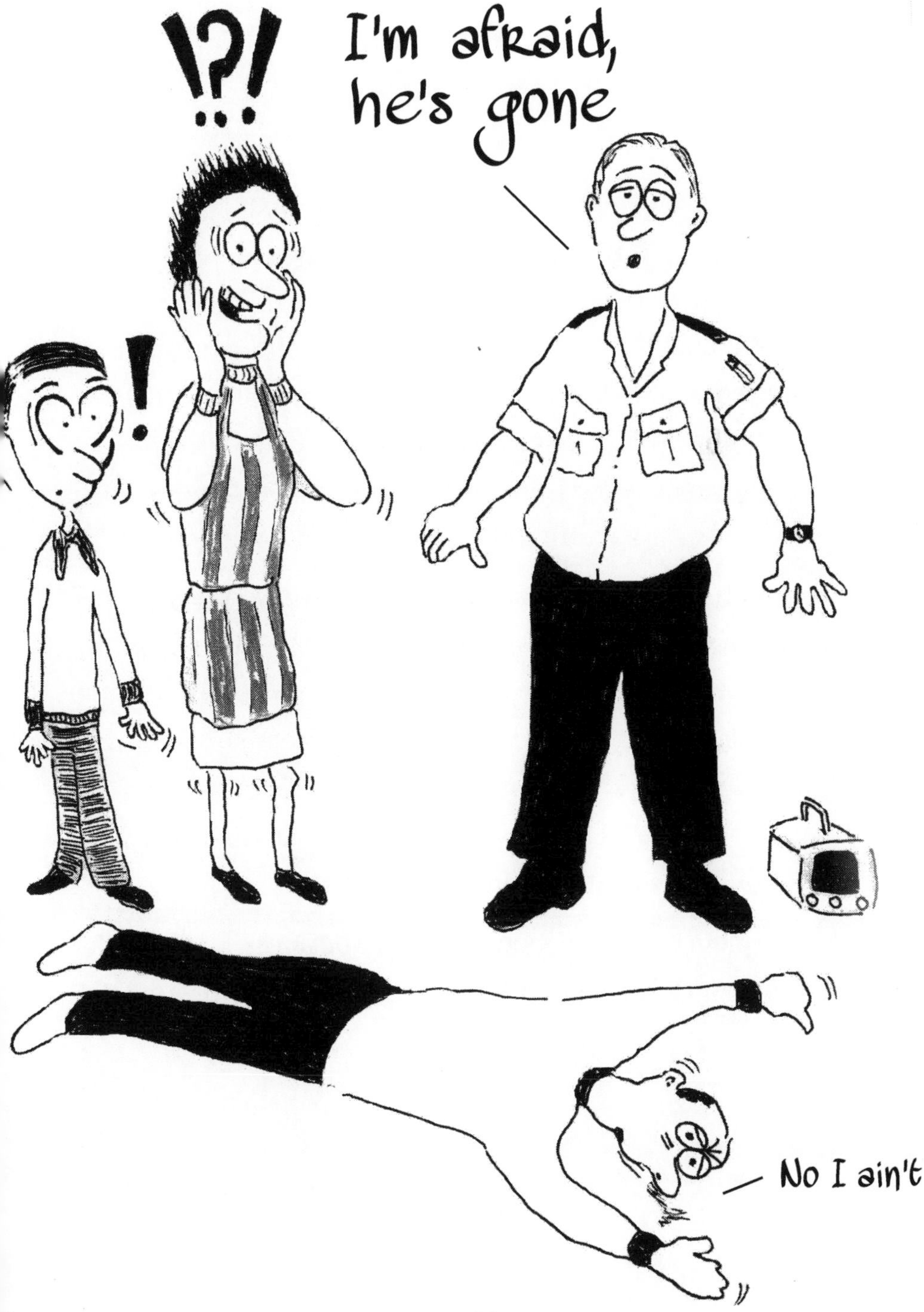
!?!
I'm afraid, he's gone
!
No I ain't

ANYTHING YOU CAN DO, I CAN DO BETTER

An ambulance was responding to a call to attend to a man reported to have had a fit and fallen. On arrival, the crew was shown upstairs to find the patient on the floor, seemingly recovering from the fit, but with cuts to his head from a piece of glass.

The crew decided to fetch a carry chair and brought the patient down the stairs. As they reached the front door they had to negotiate a dog-leg porch way, but unfortunately, the ambulance man at the foot of the chair forgot to turn the required angle and smashed through the single-paned glass porch. He lay on the floor twitching and had cuts to his head, identical to the initial call-out.

His crewmate had to call for two more ambulances, one to deal with the original call and the other to take his mate to hospital

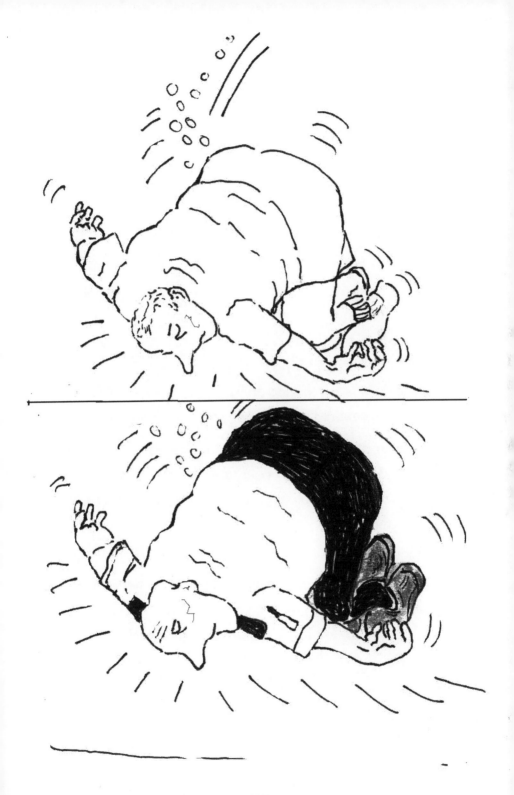

KEEPING ABREAST
OF VITAL SIGNS

As heart monitors became commonplace on ambulances during the 80s, protocol dictated that all patients who dialled 999 for an ambulance complaining of chest pain had to be monitored. Such was the case when an attractive 20-year-old female was experiencing chest pain. Although the crew believed she was suffering only a panic attack, a full set of observations naturally had to take place.

After her statistics had been very thoroughly observed and she had calmed down, her chest pain subsided. Watching this new breakthrough in ambulance procedure was the patient's 80-year-old grandmother, who after watching the crew's thorough examination declared, 'She had chest pain a fortnight ago'.

Granny's hopes of receiving a full examination herself were quickly dashed as the crew advised her to make an appointment to see her GP Monday morning.

FINAL VOYAGE

A report of an obviously-deceased male lying in the reeds and bulrushes at the side of a steep river embankment left the police and ambulance services in a quandary as to how the body could be safely retrieved on a filthy November evening.

Ropes and harnesses were considered too dangerous to haul the body up the steep, slippery embankment. So the ambulance station's plastic-coated coffin was requested and launched into the water. The body was placed in the coffin and with the assistance of the current was floated downstream by the police, to be moored and removed by the waiting ambulance staff 200 yards away.

Job done!

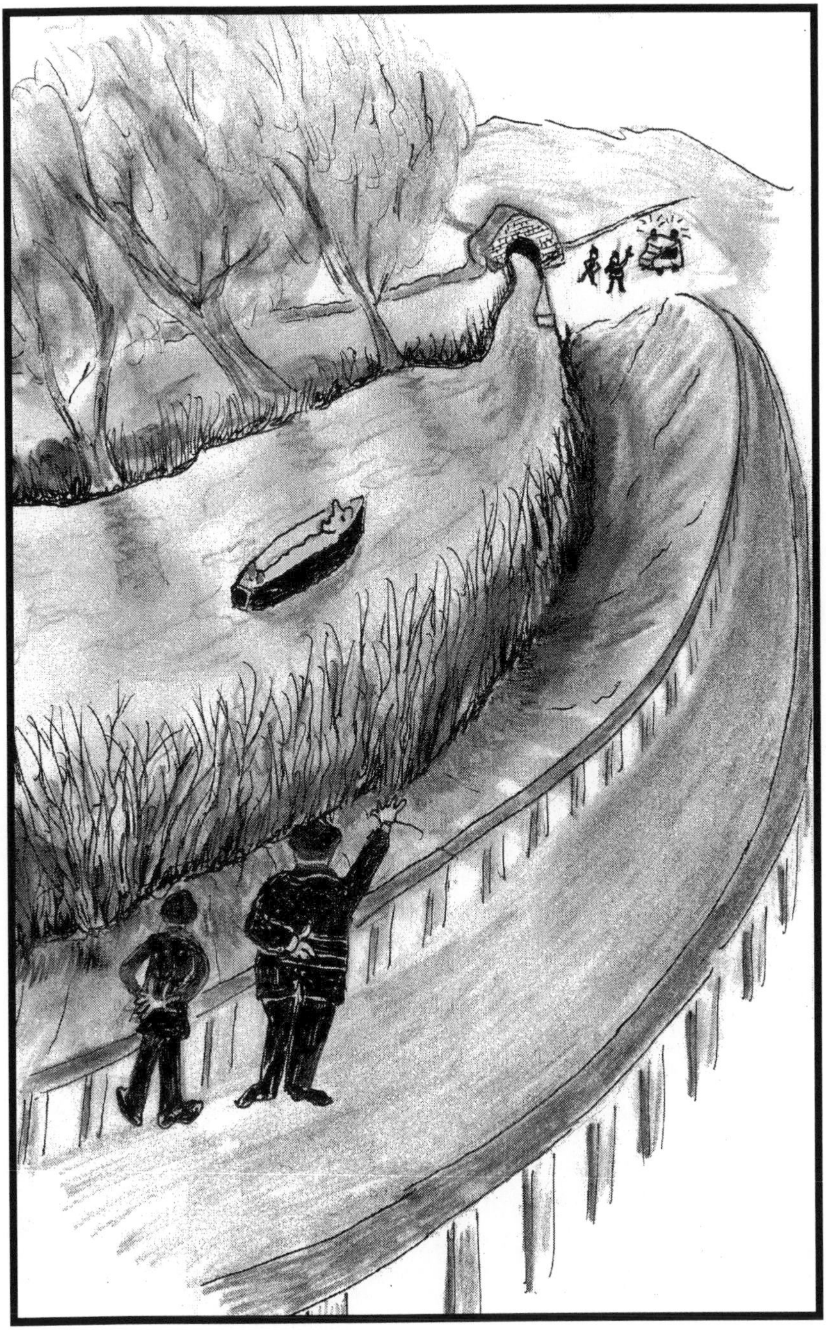

WHAT A WAY TO GO

Having been called to a male collapsed in a first floor flat, the ambulance crew made their way to the front door. They were unable to gain access, but heard frantic screams from a woman within. The crew made the decision to break the door down and followed the cries for help into the woman's bedroom.

The crew was somewhat embarrassed to find a man on top of the woman in the missionary position, the female shouting 'please get him off me!' On closer examination, it was apparent that the male had suffered some sort of seizure and had stopped breathing. The ambulance crew attempted to resuscitate him, but all their efforts were in vain and they eventually had to give up.

The crew offered their sympathies to the lady and asked for the dead man's details. There was a moment's silence before she confessed that she didn't know him. It soon became apparent the lady had flirted with the man in the pub and invited him back to her flat for sex.

The crew told the lady 'We will have to inform the police, they are very good at dealing with confidential delicate matters'.

The lady shrieked 'For God's sake no, my husband's the local beat bobby and he's off duty in an hour!'

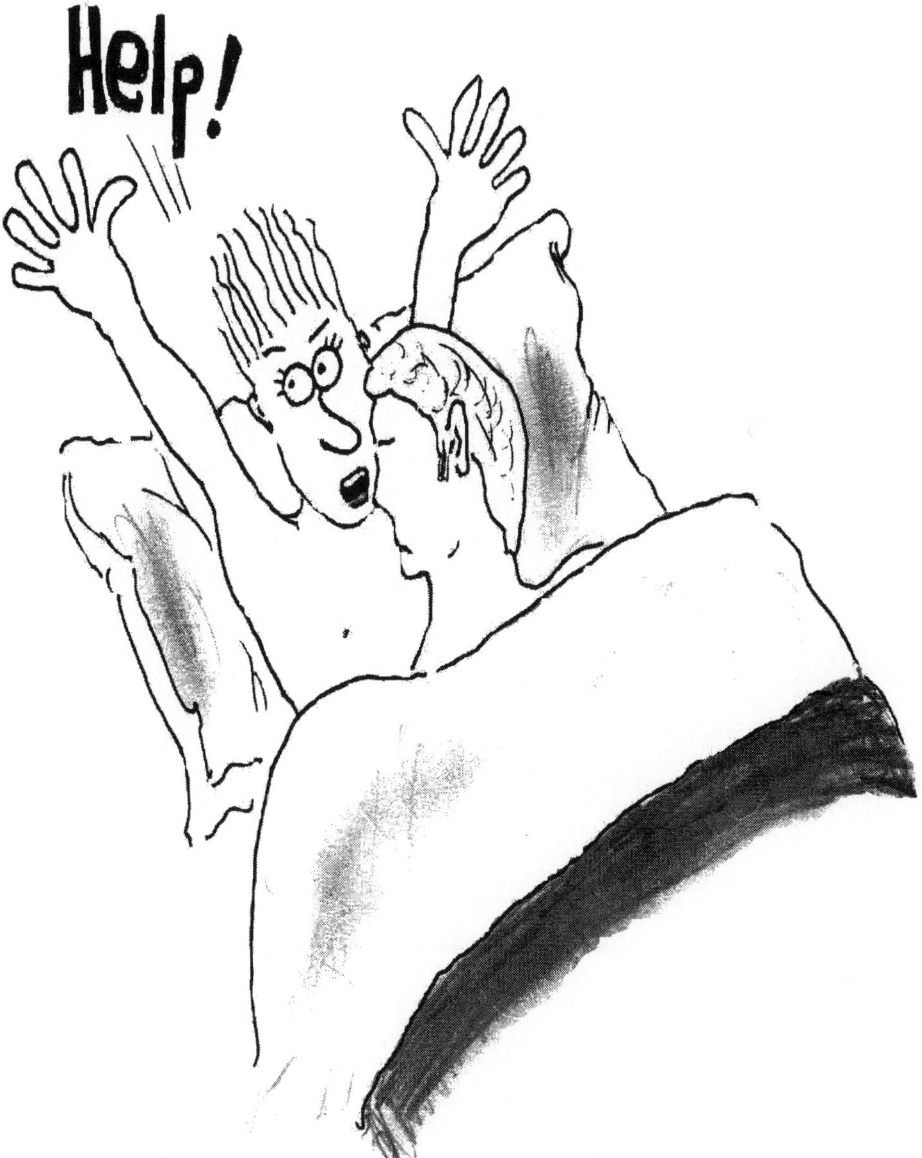
Help!

WARM RESPONSE FROM THE PUBLIC

1989 saw an unprecedented level of public support for a long and bitter national ambulance dispute which lasted over a year. Crews were extremely grateful for the generous support given by the general public. Ambulance staff would sit by burning braziers outside their station, never leaving their posts 24/7. Passing cars would sound their horns and even stop to throw money into a bucket in support of the cause.

However, on one particular afternoon shift on 'brazier watch', passing cars were frantically sounding their horns as well as making urgent gestures with their hands. The 'brazier man' sat facing the road, waving back in gratitude at the shouts and gestures from the motorists.

He was totally oblivious to the fact that fire was spreading rapidly behind him. It had burned down 200 feet of boundary fence and was creeping ever closer to the flammable oxygen storeroom.

He only realised the gravity of the situation when the fire brigade arrived to put the inferno out!

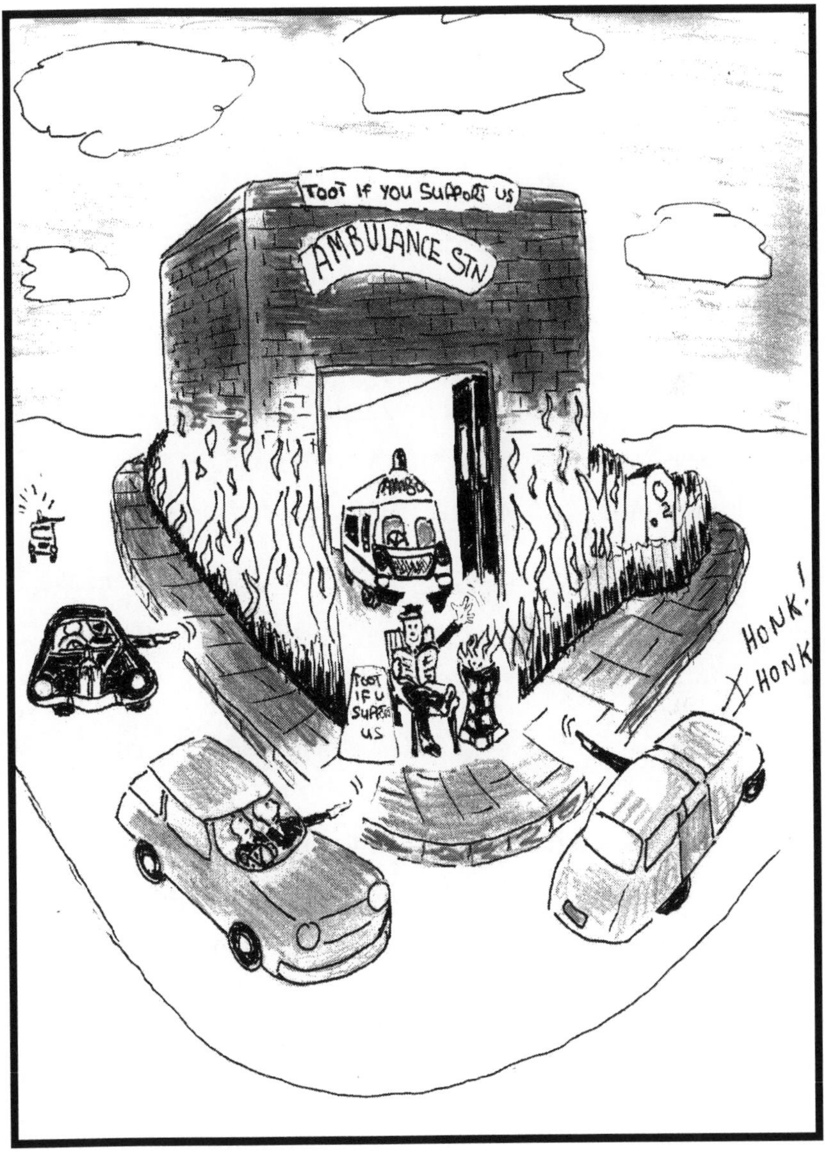
TOOT IF YOU SUPPORT US
AMBULANCE STN
AMBO
TOOT IF U SUPPORT US
HONK!
HONK

THE BUNGLING SUICIDE

Having tried on numerous occasions to 'end it all', Patrick finally decided to hang himself. He had failed many times to end his troubled life and told the attending ambulance crew that it had all started after an argument with the wife.

'I remember trying to strangle the bloke she was having an affair with, but because of the emotion of the moment, I tripped on the mat, fell over and banged my head, knocking myself out' he said. 'Then there was the time I tried to slash my wrists, but could only find a butter knife. I've cut myself worse shaving.

'Then, about six months ago, I decided to take an overdose, but some do-gooder rang for an ambulance. As it turned out, the 50 tablets I had taken were laxatives and I was running to the bog every half hour for three days.

'Finally, today, I decided to hang myself. So I got hold of a thick rope, tied it to the top of the balcony, placed a perfect hangman's noose around my neck, placed my well-worded suicide note on the table in the front bedroom, positioned myself on top of the balcony and jumped.

'How was I to know, the bloody rope was too long and I would end up with two sprained ankles?'

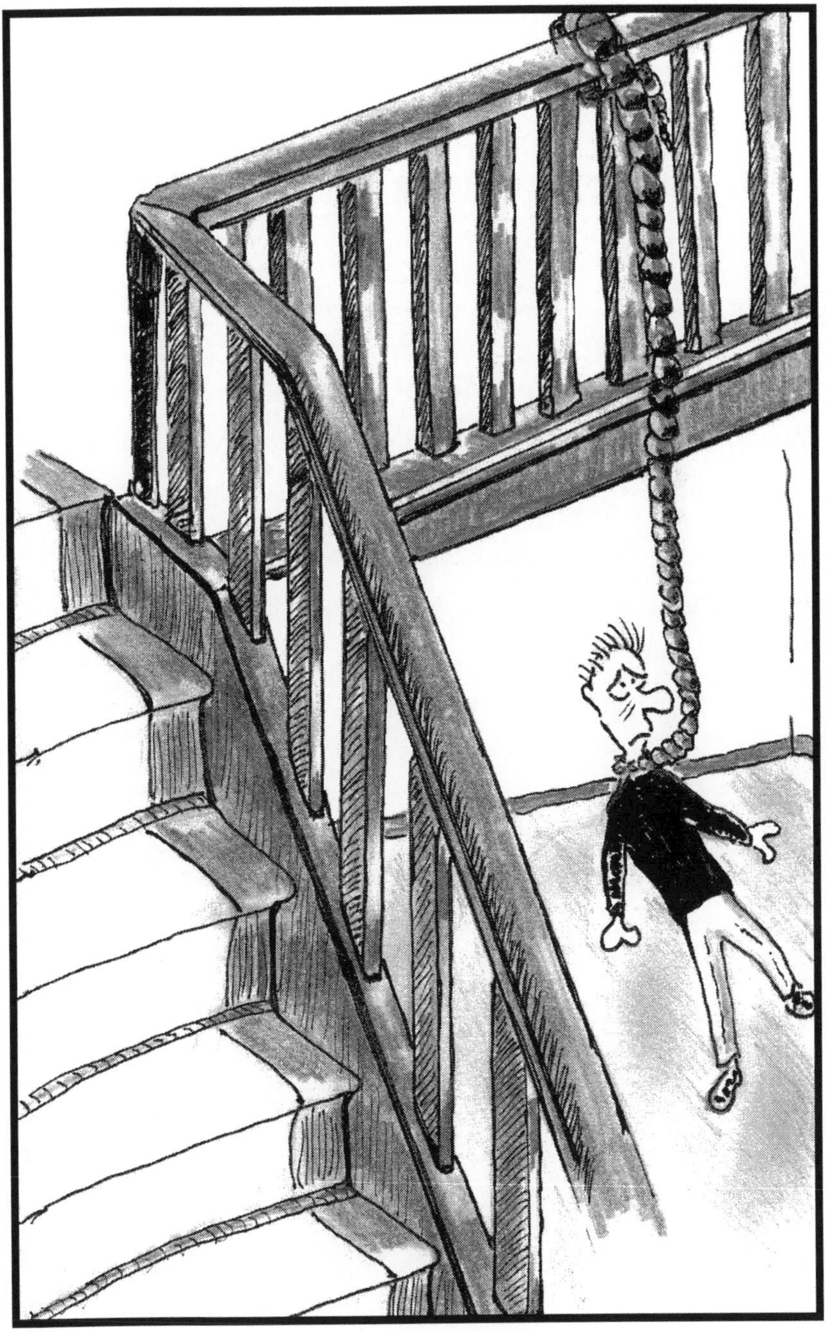

FREE SUN ROOF CONVERSION

Six weeks away from retirement, PC 691 was called to a lady who had fallen off her push bike. She was found sitting on the grass verge, seemingly uninjured. The officer beckoned the lady to sit in his brand new panda car, and she was grateful for the warmth and comfort of the passenger seat.

On arrival of the ambulance, the crew gathered a history and discovered the patient was now experiencing stiffness in her neck and was in recovery from a recent back operation. The crew said they now had to call for the assistance of the fire brigade to take the police car's roof off!

The fire brigade arrived and were briefed, and the roof was duly cut off. The patient was boarded, collared, extricated from the vehicle and placed on a stretcher. PC 691 was wondering what kind of report he could submit to pacify his boss when the scene was further compromised by vehicles travelling in the opposite direction, colliding into each other - due to the unusual sight of an open-top police car.

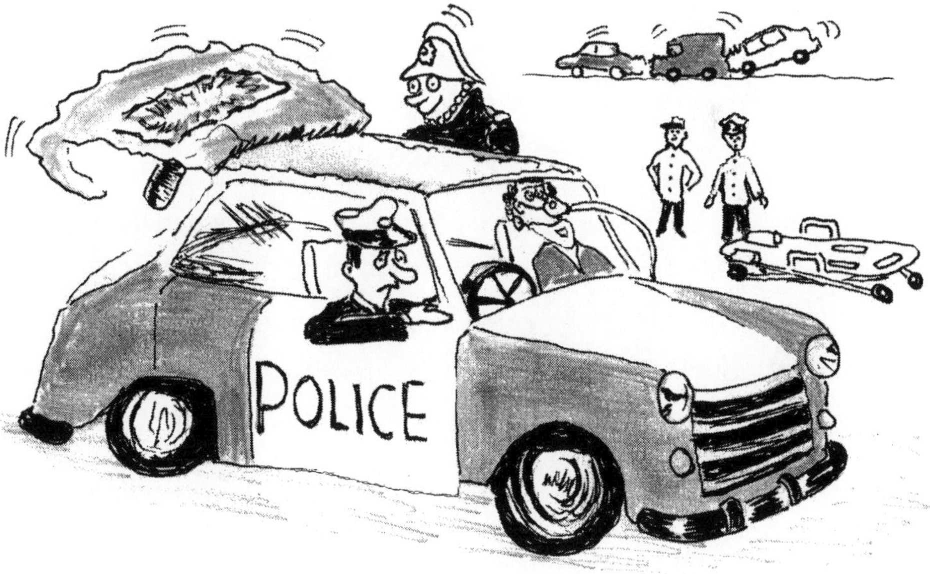
POLICE

HOW TO LOSE SEVEN PATIENTS

It should have been an uneventful trip to the psycho-geriatric hospital as seven elderly mentally-infirm patients were picked up and dropped off by ambulance at the day unit. On arrival, the patients disembarked and the driver parked the vehicle in the ambulance bay. The attendant herded the patients into the reception area and waited for the lift to take them for their appointment on the third floor.

One of the patients became anxious because he had left his walking stick on the ambulance, so the attendant went back to the vehicle to fetch it, momentarily leaving the patients unattended. At just that time the lift arrived, and all seven patients, like a flock of sheep, boarded the lift.

On the return of the ambulance crew some 20 seconds later, they had managed to lose all seven. Both crew members pressed lift buttons and started frantically running up and down the stairs to find them.

In almost pathetic desperation, the crew of the 'missing seven' sheepishly went to tell sister. They walked past the day room to find all seven patients sitting around a table drinking tea.

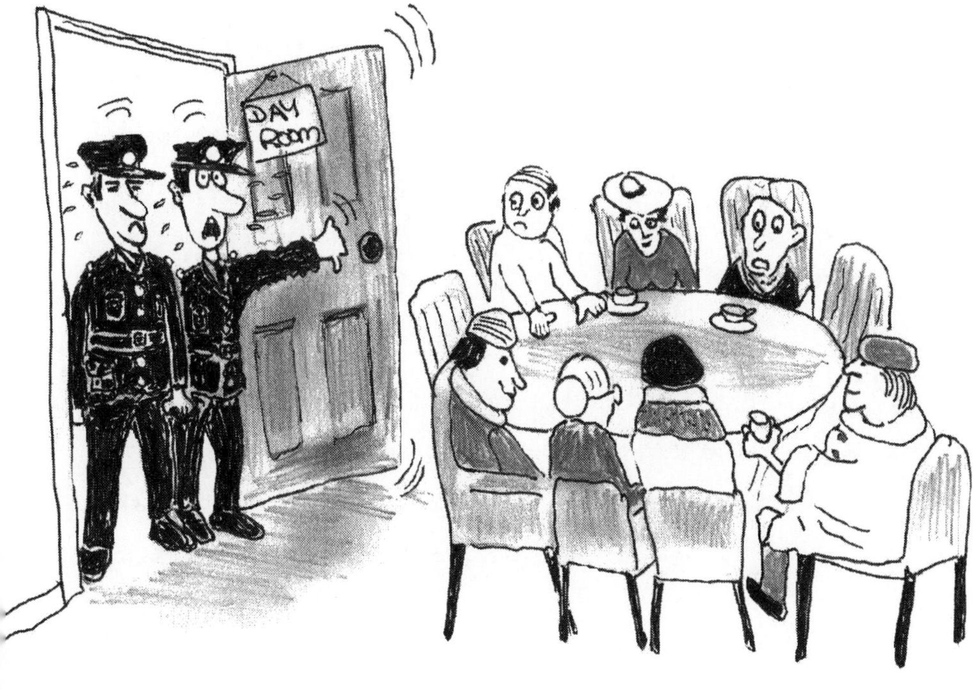
DAY
Room

SHE ADDER NASTY SHOCK...

A female outpatient who lived in a high-rise flat had the misfortune to have suffered from mental illness over a number of years. She would go to her psychiatric day unit clinic five days a week, transported there and back by the routine ambulance service.

She was making excellent progress, until one day she decided to run to the corner shop to purchase a loaf of bread just before the ambulance arrived. In the short amount of time she was out of her flat, a large adder managed to escape from an upstairs neighbour's vivarium, slither through the communal pipework and find a comfortable seat in the front living room, where she found it happily watching daytime TV!

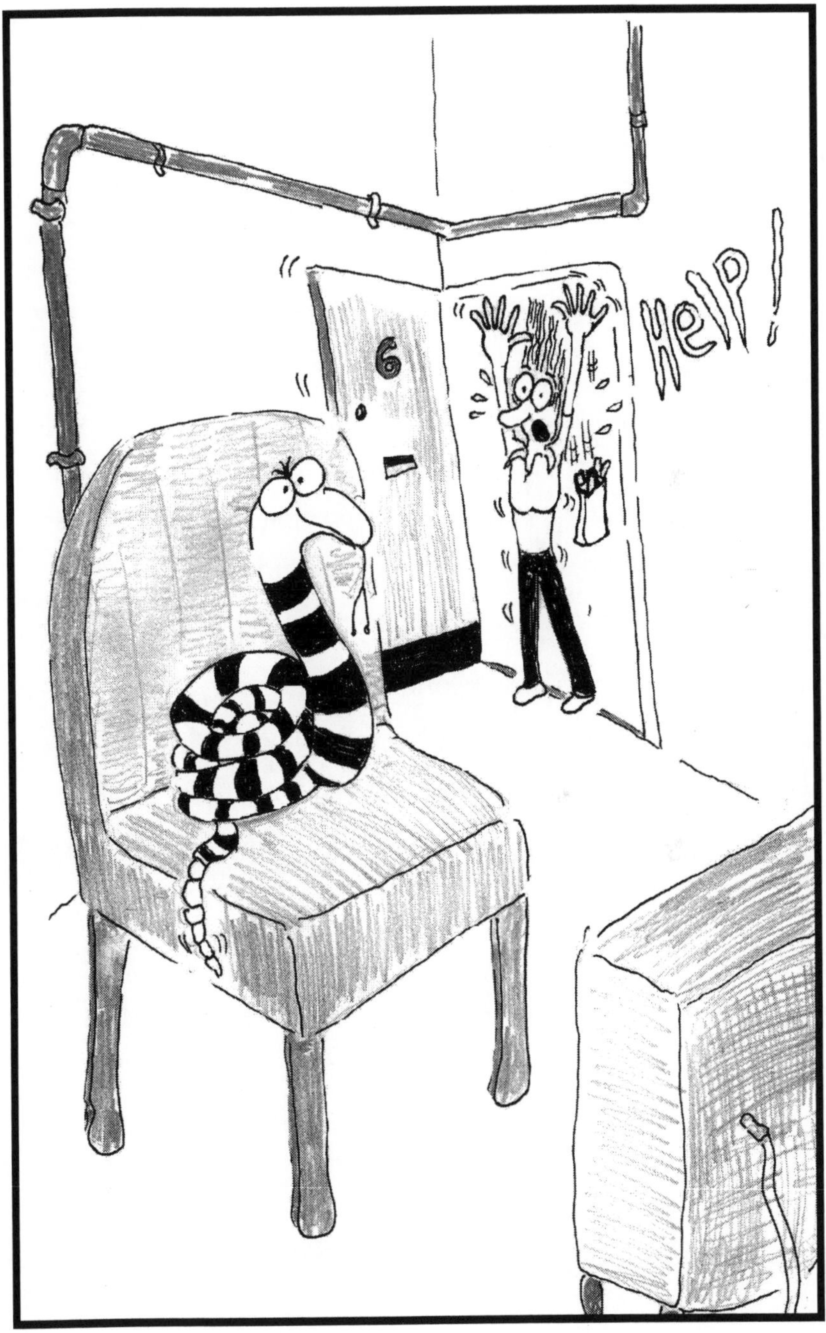
6
HelP!

THE RIGHT SIGNATURE TUNE

Responding solo to a cardiac arrest can be a daunting enough experience, but when the information passed reveals that it's your old ambulance boss who's in trouble, the need to get everything right is of paramount importance.

Resuscitation took place immediately on arrival, and an ambulance crew arrived seconds after the solo responder. As the crew were setting up various pieces of equipment, the responder performed cardiac compression. If he was in any doubt as to the timing of his cardiac compressions he need not have worried, as his mobile phone went off - in perfect compression timing - to the ringtone of the BBC series Casualty.

A tiny bit embarrassing!

OUT OF THE FRYING PAN...

On the nightshift, before sat nav and vehicle location systems were on ambulances, crews would often take a detour through the city centre to the chip shop to get their supper when returning to base. One night, just before the ambulance arriving at the chippy, a car in front decided to stop and perform what the crew thought was a three-point turn. The ambulance stopped to allow the driver to complete the manoeuvre.

After completing the first part of the turn, the car revved its engine and reversed straight into a jewellers. A ram raid took place in direct view of the crew.

The quick-thinking ambulance driver moved his vehicle in front of the ram raid vehicle in an attempt to block it in, not realising that a getaway team were waiting in a second car facing the opposite way. The jewellery was stuffed into a bag, thrown into the back of the second vehicle and driven away, leaving the crew having to report to control not only what had happened, but also what they were doing there in the first place!

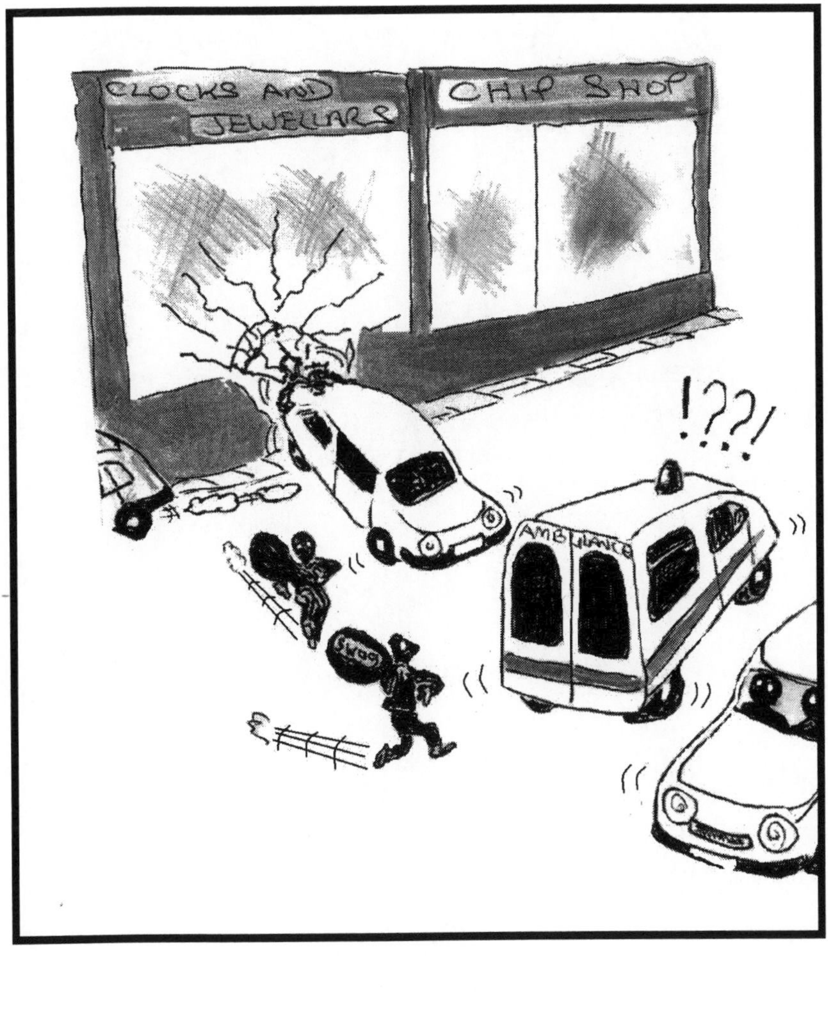
CLOCKS AND JEWELLARS
CHIP SHOP
!???!
AMBULANCE

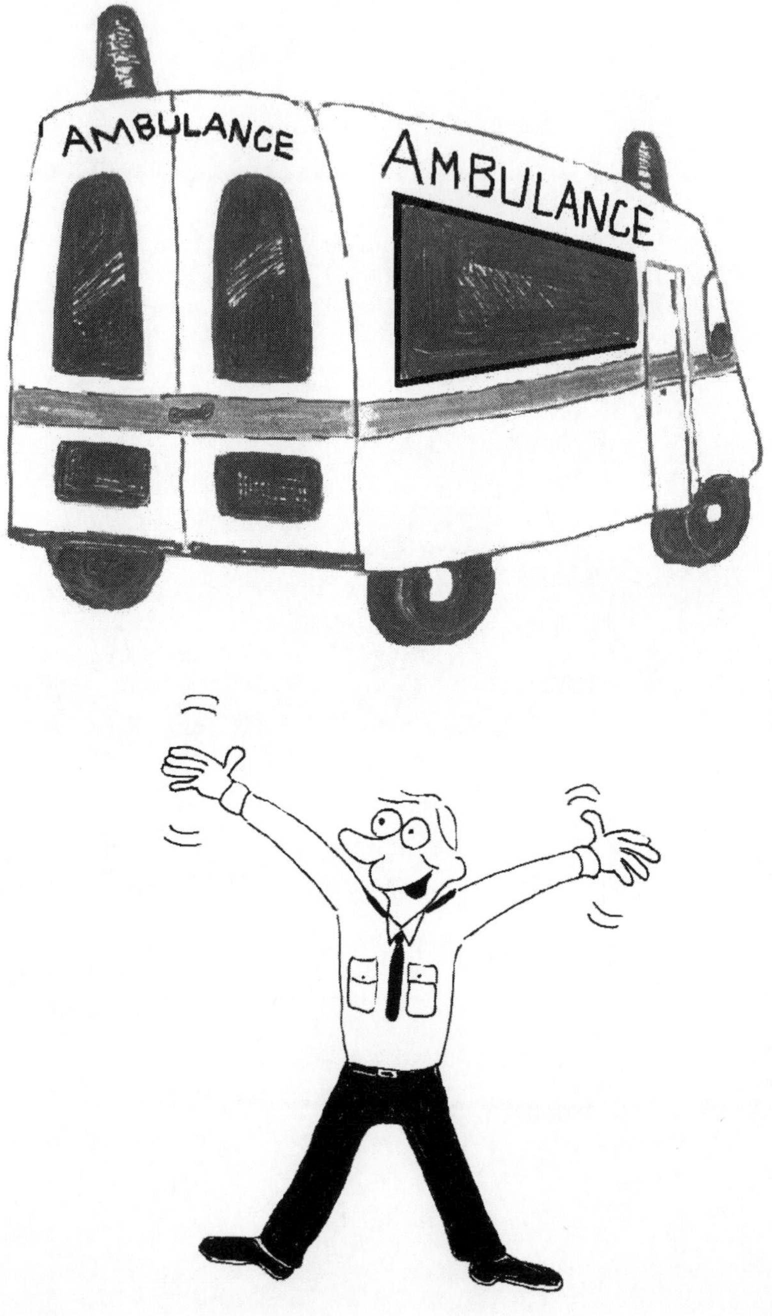
AMBULANCE
AMBULANCE

THE 1990'S

TANKS FOR NOTHING

BONUS BABY

HE'S FINE, APART FROM THE MISSING HEAD

ALL GRASSED UP

GOOD VIBRATIONS

LIVE ON CAMERA

PUTTING HIS FOOT IN IT

CROSS-DRESSING CONFUSION

SELF-SUSTAINED INJURY

DIFFICULTY IN BREATHING, SIR?

WHAT A WAY TO GO

I DEMAND A SECOND OPINION

YOU'RE NOT SUPPOSED TO PULL THEIR LEGS OFF!

TOILET IN USE

THE PINOCCHIO TREATMENT

BELLY LAUGH

NO SMOKE WITHOUT FIRE

PLEASE RELEASE ME, LET ME GO...

NO POINT IN GOING HOME

EXTERMINATE, EXTERMINATE!

HOLD ON, I'M COMING

TANKS FOR NOTHING

On arrival at the address where they'd been sent, the crew found that the patient's pride and joy was a huge marine aquarium, 12 feet wide, holding 1000 litres of temperature-controlled water. Although the patient was suffering from shortage of breath, he managed to boast about the different types of fish in his tank, detailing the eating and mating habits of clown fish, sea horses and angel fish.

All very interesting, but it was time to put the patient on a carry chair, place him on oxygen and off to hospital. A small oxygen bottle was placed on the carry chair's crossbar and the patient was carried from his bedroom and down the stairs.

All was going well until the oxygen bottle slid off the carry chair and thumped into the centre of the fish tank. Everyone held their breath as the tank seemed to hold together, but then a crack appeared, followed by 1000 litres of water crashing to the floor like a mini tsunami. More than £3000 worth of exotic fish were now flipping helplessly on the living-room carpet.

The crew cringed with embarrassment, lost for words, until one of them made the unhelpful statement, 'I should put them in some water mate'. The journey to hospital was very frosty!

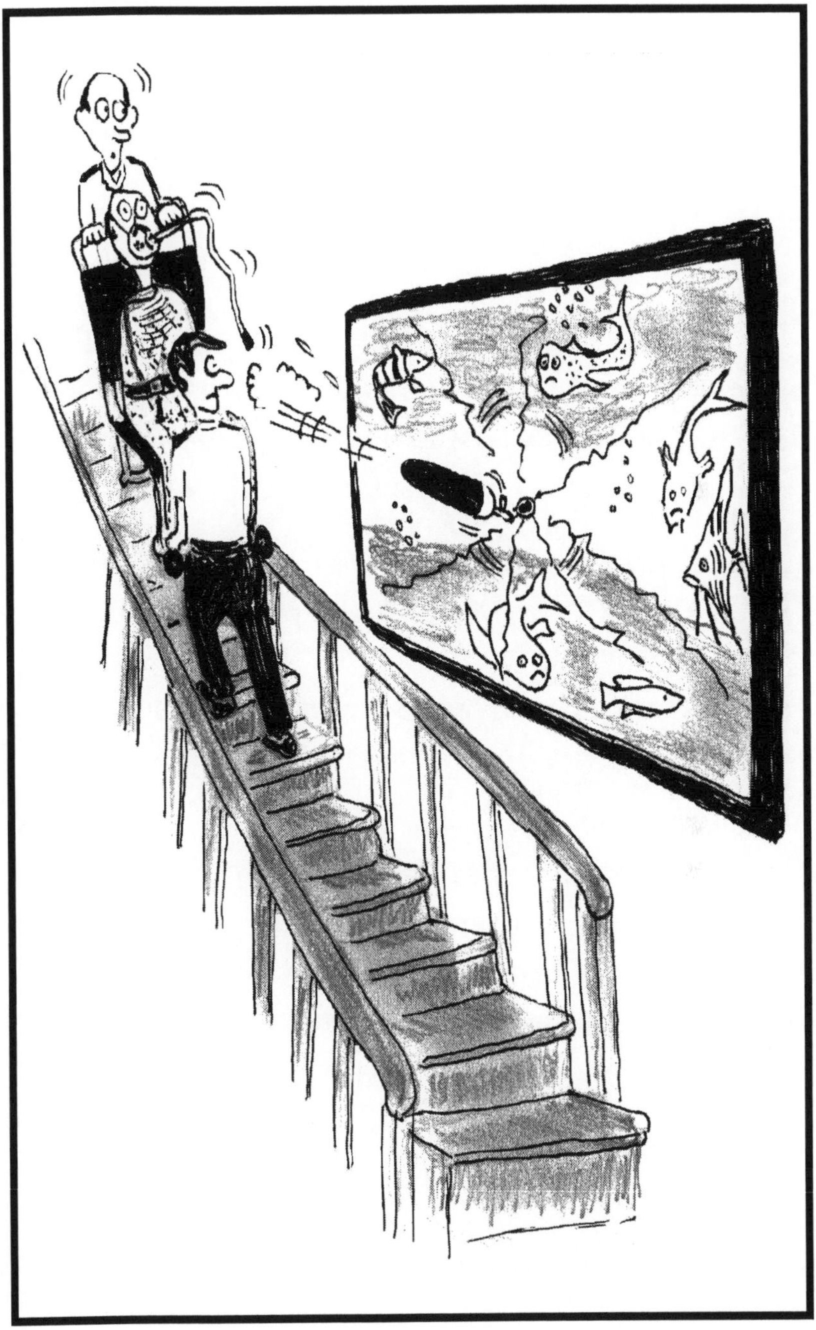

BONUS BABY

A crew was called to a block of flats to attend a young girl with abdominal pains, who kept saying she had the urge to push. To say the flat was a dump would be an understatement. There were eight puppies running amok, and dog mess lay in all corners of every room.

The young female (who we shall call Mercedes) was 17 years old and already had a two-year-old daughter. The female paramedic asked her if she was pregnant. She replied, 'Nah, cos I'm on pill injection, innit.'

The contraception obviously wasn't working, as she then went into labour and pushed out a gorgeous tiny baby girl. Mercedes was shocked but delighted at the same time, as she excitedly rang her partner, who was out collecting his dole. She announced 'Babe, you'll never guess wot, you're a dad and the council will 'ave to give us a three-bedroomed house!'

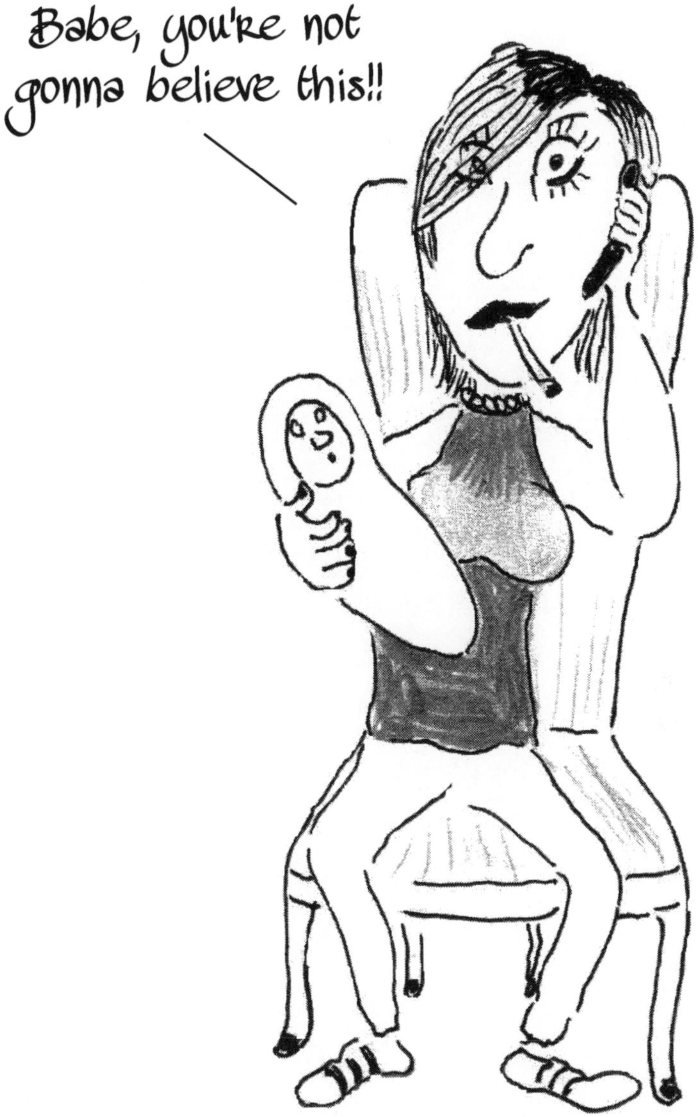
Babe, you're not gonna believe this!!

HE'S FINE, APART FROM THE MISSING HEAD

Ambulance crews have to deal with some horrible sights. Such was the case when a man decided to end it all by jumping off a bridge in front of an oncoming train. When the ambulance arrived, they saw that the patient had been decapitated.

The crew placed the deceased in a body bag and placed the head in a separate bag. They labelled the bags and waited for the railway police to carry out a preliminary investigation before the doctor turned out to certify death.

When the quirky old doc arrived, the crew showed him the deceased body and the doctor asked 'Has the patient got any other injuries?'

As if a head separated from a body just wasn't enough.

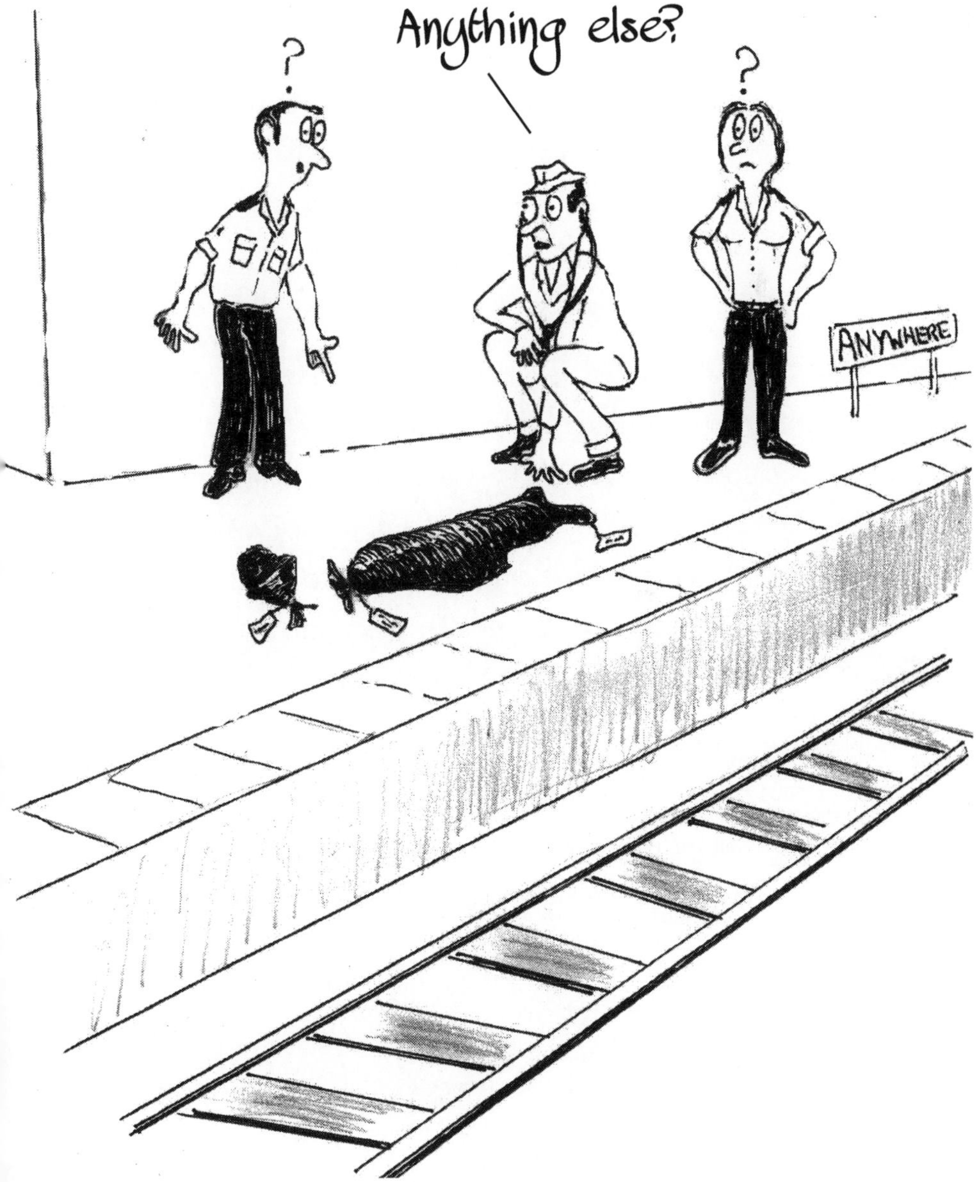
?
Anything else?
?
ANYWHERE

ALL GRASSED UP

Having arrived at the day unit to take home eight geriatrics, the patients started to get all excited, knowing that an ambulance helicopter was about to land. It was to touch down behind the hospital's cricket pitch, a mere 300 yards from where the ambulance was parked.

As the patients had never seen a landing before, the ambulance driver agreed that they could all watch the landing and positioned the vehicle to give them the best vantage point. The back and side doors of the ambulance were opened to allow all patients to have a good view. Two of the patients even stood at the rear of the vehicle, resting on their zimmer frames, to get a better look.

As the helicopter made its descent, it became obvious that the wet grass had only recently been cut. As it landed all eight patients were covered from head to toe in grass cuttings, blown towards the ambulance by the rotor blades.

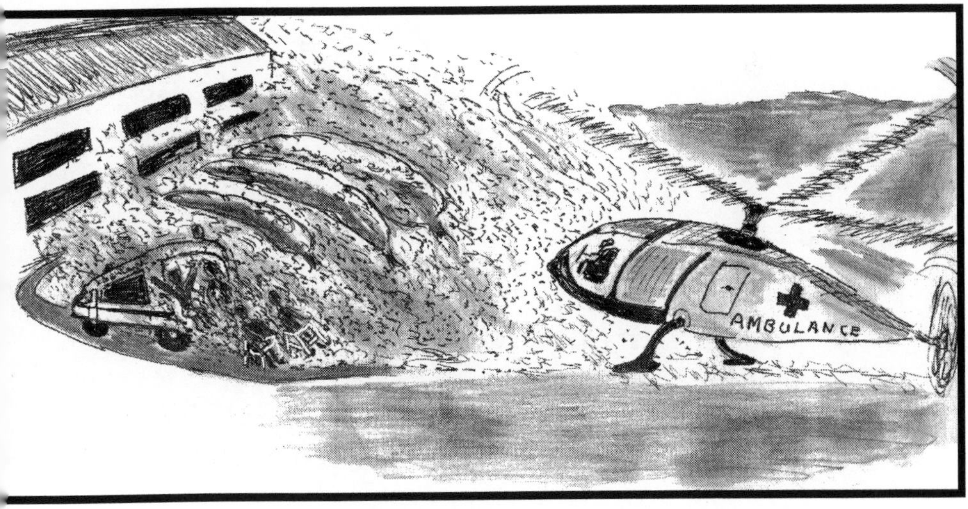
AMBULANCE

GOOD VIBRATIONS

An ambulance crew was given a doctor's urgent request to take a 70-year-old lady into hospital suffering from shortage of breath. The ambulance arrived too early, and the patient was not ready for the pending journey, so the crew offered to help her and gathered her comb, flannel, soap and toothbrush. 'My nightie is under the pillow' she said. When the ambulance man reached for her nightie, out came a huge vibrator.

'Should I pack this too?' said the embarrassed ambulance man. 'Yes please' came the reply. She went on to tell him that she had trouble sleeping at night and even counting sheep wasn't working.

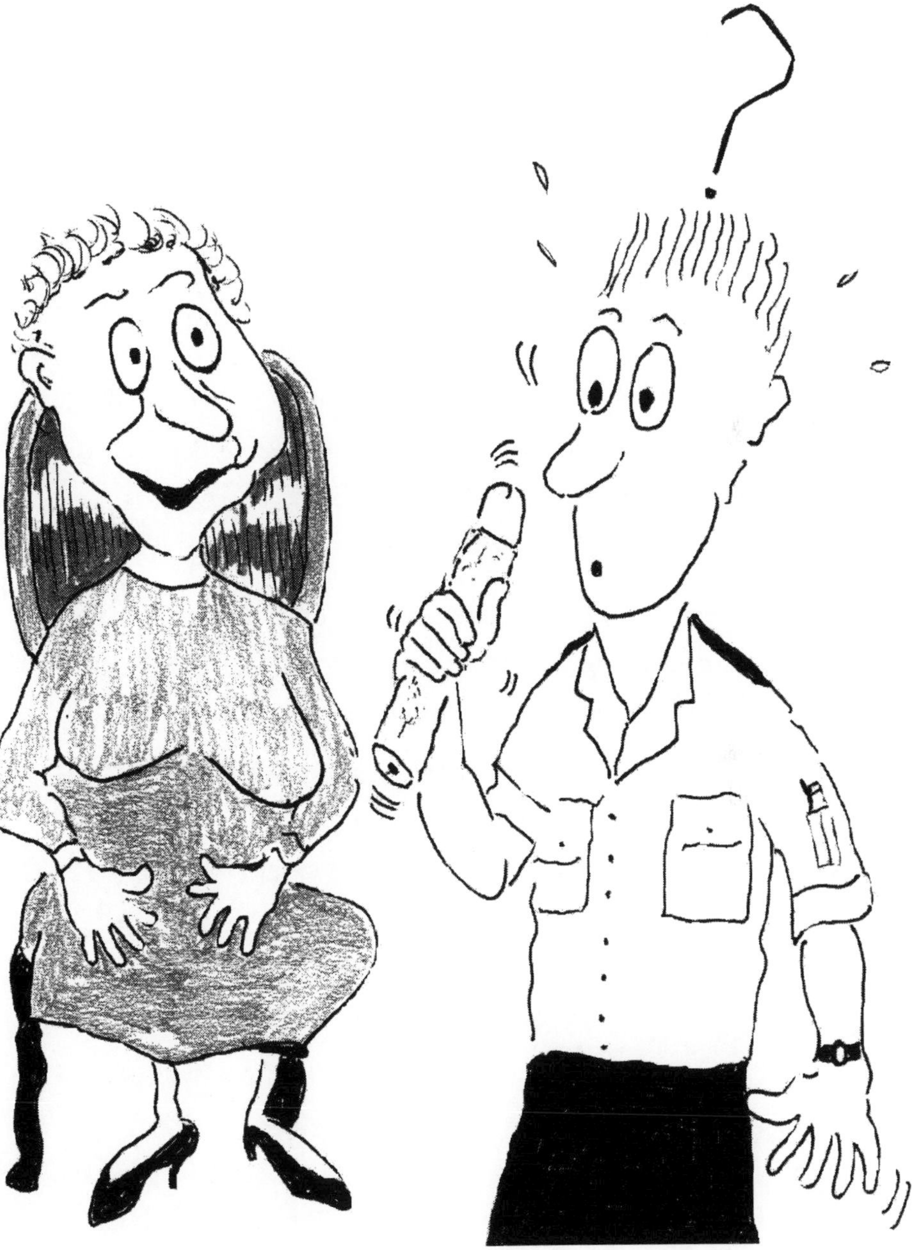

LIVE ON CAMERA

In the early 1990s the BBC ran a live broadcast covering the work of the emergency ambulance service. As well as going out with ambulance crews on the road, great interest was also generated in the running of the ambulance control room.

As the female control assistant received an emergency call, about a patient who was having a heart attack, she quickly turned round and started running to pass the details to the ambulance controller, momentarily forgetting the live camera was right behind her. She smacked into it with such force that she needed an ambulance herself.

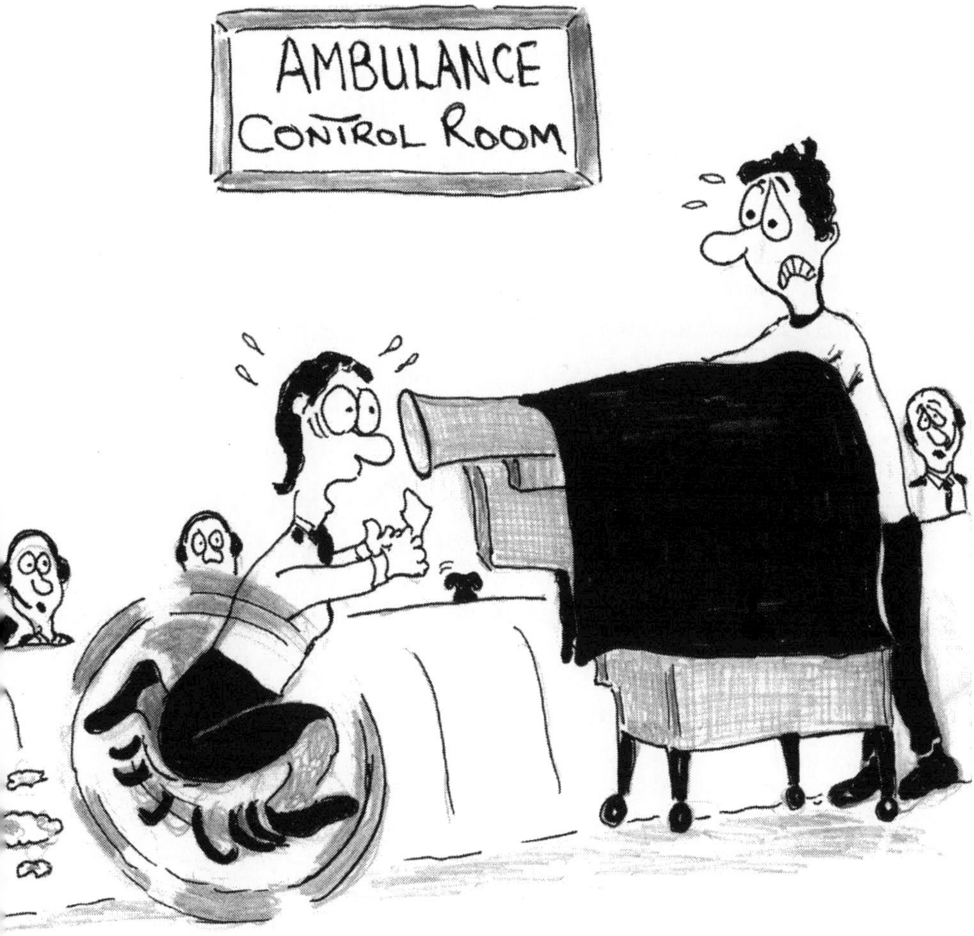
AMBULANCE
CONTROL ROOM

PUTTING HIS FOOT IN IT

A crew attending a 999 call to a young offenders' institution were directed to a medical ward to find a young man who had put his foot through a bottle-shaped glass window. He had cut his ankle so badly that he had almost cut his foot off.

The patient had already been handcuffed to two prison officer escorts. He was taken by carry chair to the ambulance and placed on a stretcher, still attached to the two prison officers. The almost-severed foot was then placed in a box splint for support.

The crew took the patient and the two attached prison officers to the local casualty, where a team of medical staff received the entourage. The doctor asked the crew 'how bad is the cut?' to which they replied, 'It's not a cut, it's almost an amputation'.

The doctor took hold of the patient's foot, held the big toe and brought the whole of the almost severed foot up to the patient's shin. As he performed this manoeuvre, one of the prison officers fainted. In doing so he dragged the patient off the trolley, breaking the wrist of the other officer.

Neither prison officer had keys to undo the handcuffs, so the fire brigade was called to cut them free, allowing all three patients to receive treatment.

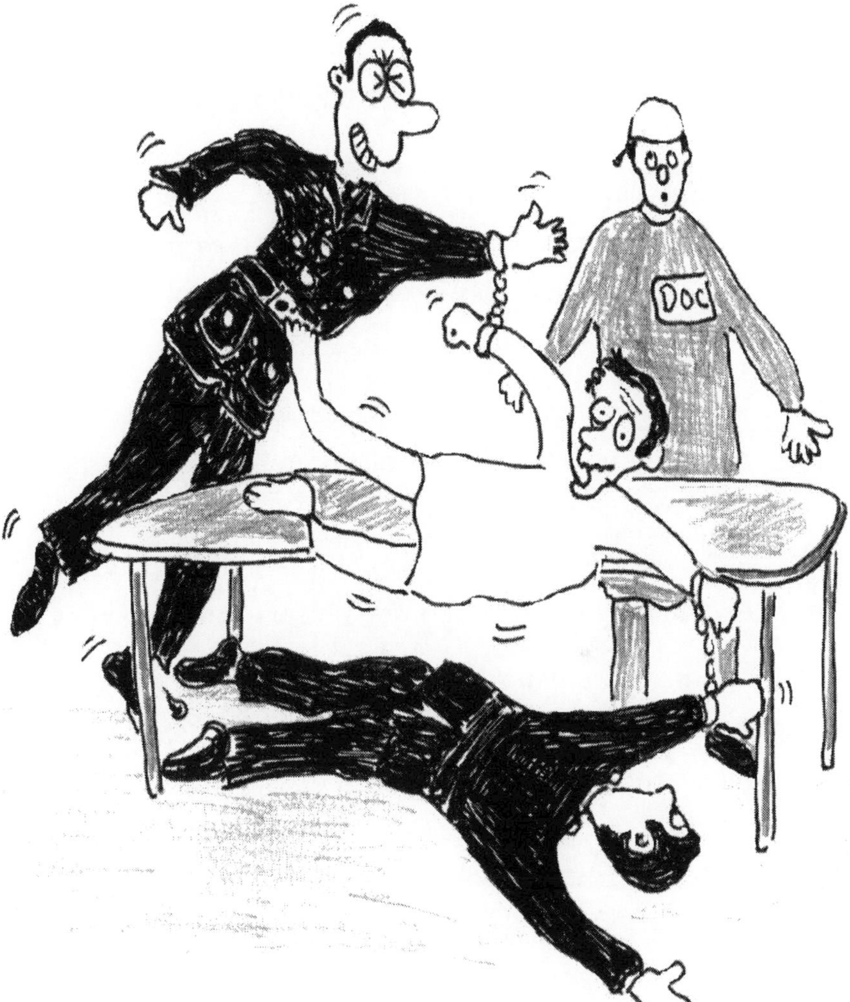
DOC

CROSS-DRESSING CONFUSION

A crew was called to attend a man of about 30 years of age who had slashed his wrist following a drunken argument with his boyfriend. On arrival they were met by the boyfriend, who said, 'Sandra's in the toilet.'

The crew was confused, as they had been told the patient was male. They entered the loo, and all became clear when they saw that 'Sandra' was a transvestite. 'She' was sitting on the trap with a huge Adams apple, a mini skirt and a large set of male equipment hanging out of the side of her torn fishnets.

Having bandaged 'Sandra's' wrist, it was time to place her on a stretcher and take 'her' off to hospital, but not before the ambulance man had got her tatty blonde wig stuck in one of his press studs, and ripped it clean off, revealing a bald head. The more he tried to unpick the knots, the more it got tangled, to the obvious amusement of his colleague.

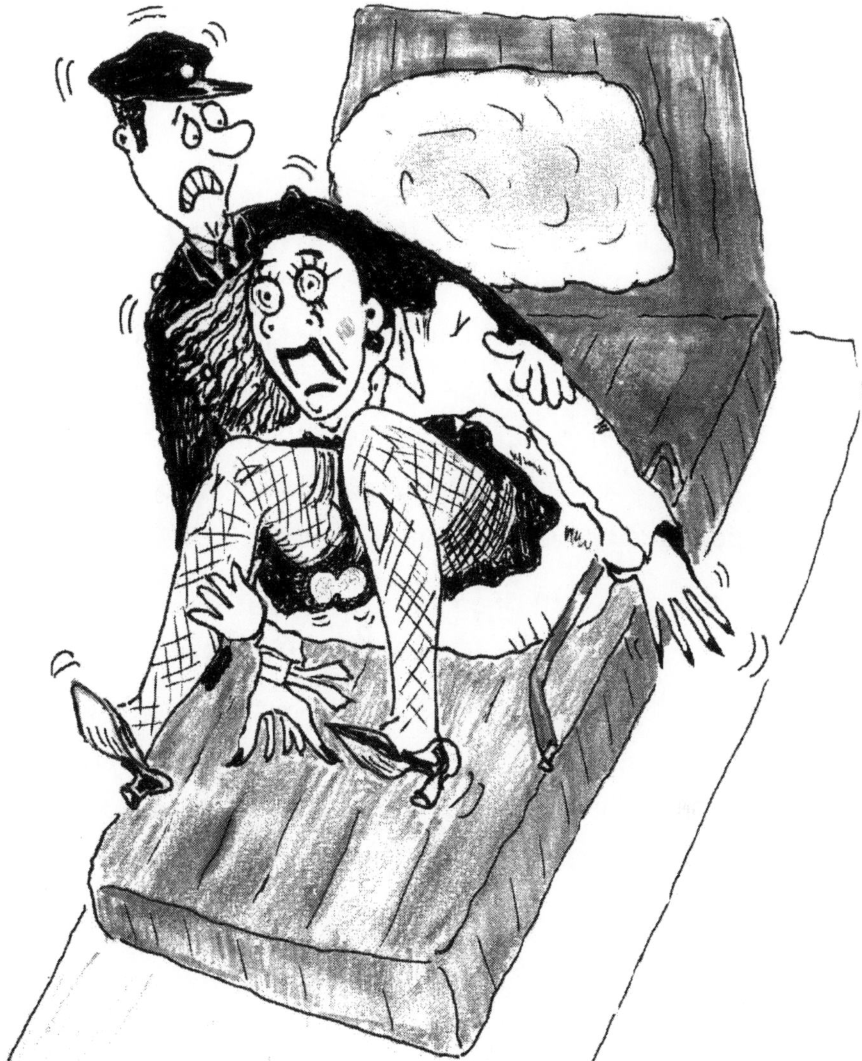

SELF-SUSTAINED INJURY

Reg, a retained fire officer for his area, was fortunate enough to own two cars. His son was going to a rock concert one night and asked Dad if he could borrow one of them. After the usual family quarrel about driving too fast and who was going to pay for the petrol, Reg gave in, and off went the lad in one of his cars.

About an hour later, Reg took a call given as a vehicle entrapment and made his way quickly to the fire station, while the fire crew went off to attend. On arrival, Reg instantly recognised his own car down in a ditch. Fortunately his lad was sitting on the side of the road, unhurt, though in shock. However, his mate was trapped in the passenger seat and complaining of neck pain.

In consultation with the attending ambulance crew, Reg had to make the agonising decision to cut the roof off his own car.

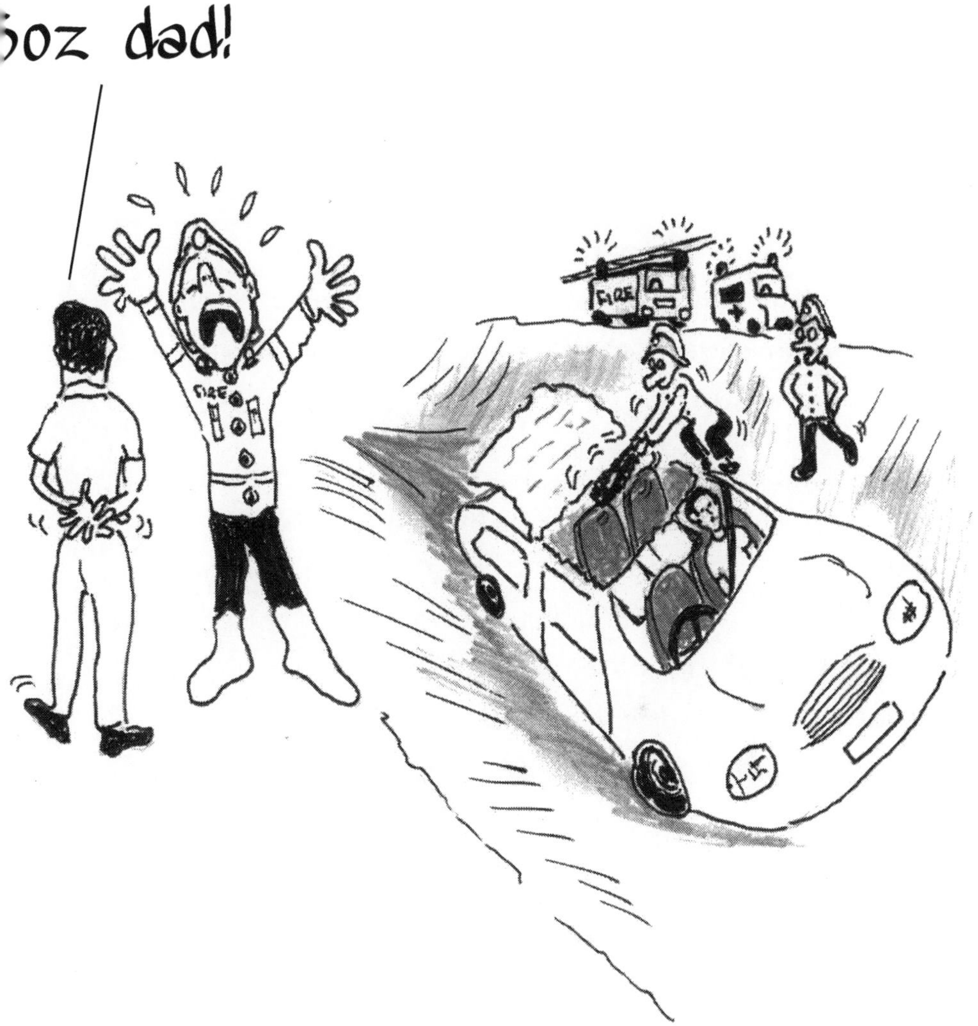

oz dad!
FIRE
FIRE

DIFFICULTY IN BREATHING, SIR?

On arrival at a patient's home, a crew was directed to a man sitting upright in a chair, suffering from breathing problems. The paramedic decided that it would be a good idea to listen to the patient's chest with a stethoscope, while his crew mate carried out further observations.

The main obstacle to listening to the patient's chest was the enormous quantity of clothing he was wearing. The paramedic peeled off the layers of clothing down to a final undergarment. He started yanking the vest in an upward direction, in an attempt to finally expose the chest. Following these actions, the patient's breathing appeared to become even more laboured.

It was only then that the crewman realised that he had been trying to pull up an all-in-one undergarment. He had given the patient an enormous wedgy, which was the main cause of his increased respiration rate!

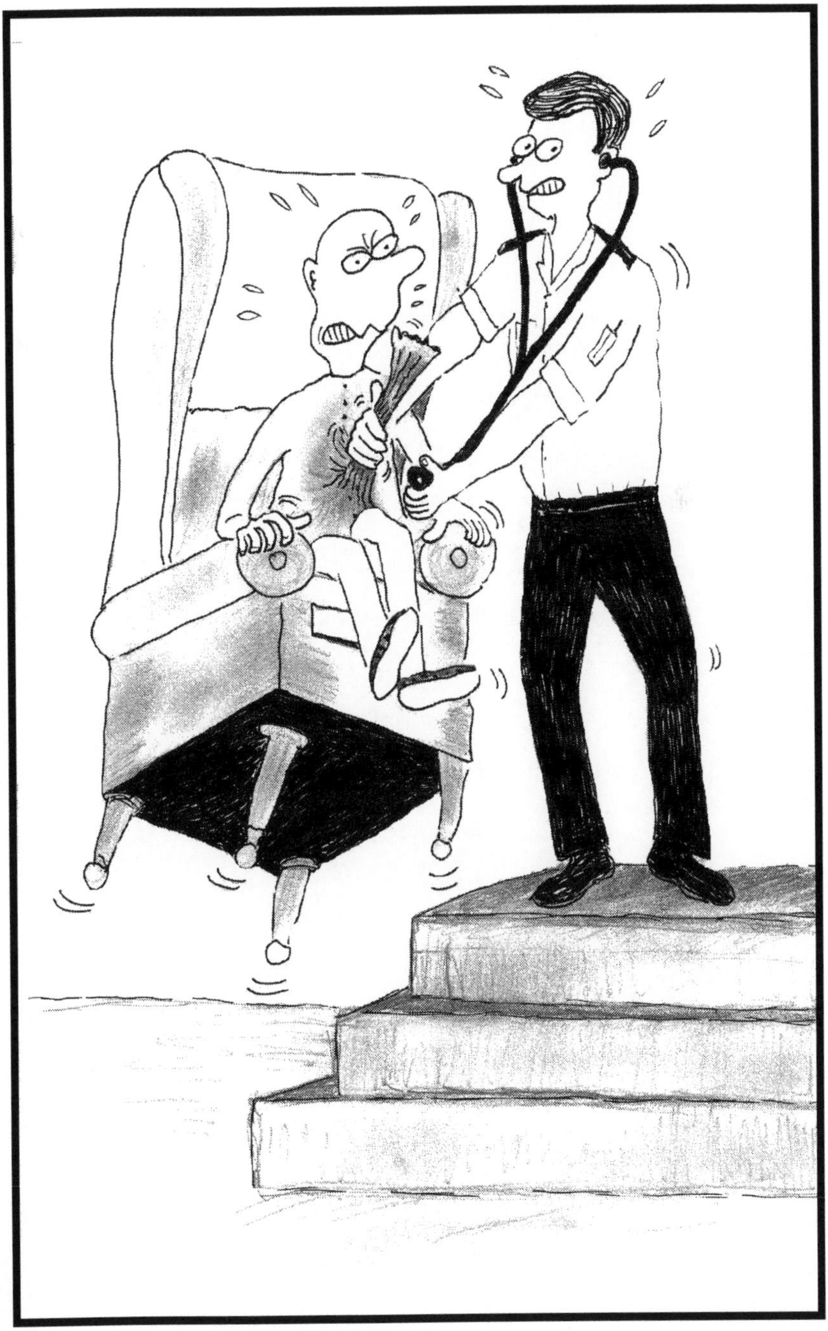

WHAT A WAY TO GO

Having attended to an elderly, poorly patient with difficulty in breathing, the male crew member gave the oxygen and bag and mask to his ample-breasted female crewmate, who assisted the patient back to consciousness by holding his hand and mopping his brow.

All the way to hospital, the patient was on oxygen, gazing into the ambulance lady's big beautiful brown eyes. On arrival he was safely placed in the resuscitation department, where he made a reasonable recovery.

On the recovery ward two days later, he was asked by the hospital to fill in a questionaire about the "patient experience"

He simply put on the form, "When I was in the ambulance, I thought I had died and gone to heaven".

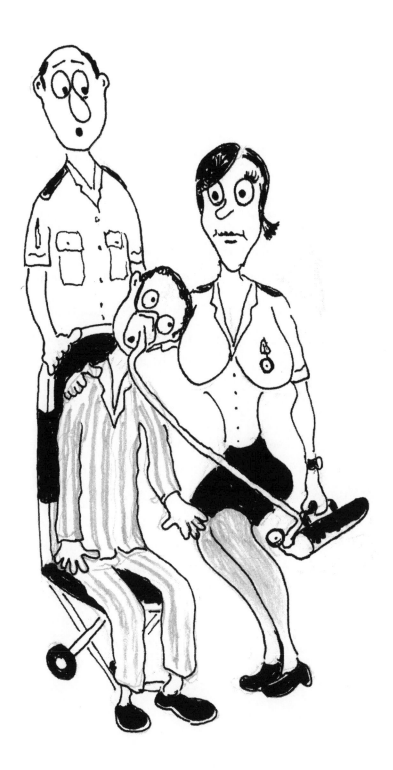

I DEMAND A SECOND OPINION

Attending a maternity case at 3 am usually just means providing ambulance transport. But on entering one house on such a call the crew found Mum with legs akimbo, greeting the crew with a high-pitched scream of 'It's coming!'

The crew members realised that they were about to pop their maternity cherry. As the baby's head was presented and Mum pushed a little harder, out came this slippery creature. One crewman nearly fainted at the site, while his mate was left literally holding the baby.

Mum asked 'what is it?' Still on an adrenaline rush, the ambulance man looked down to see what he thought was a scrotum. 'It's a boy!' he exclaimed. But just after the parents named him, he had to admit that he hadn't looked properly. 'No wait, it's a girl' he said. Fortunately the news did manage to make their day, as they had always wanted a girl. They just had to wait a minute longer to learn that their wishes had come true.

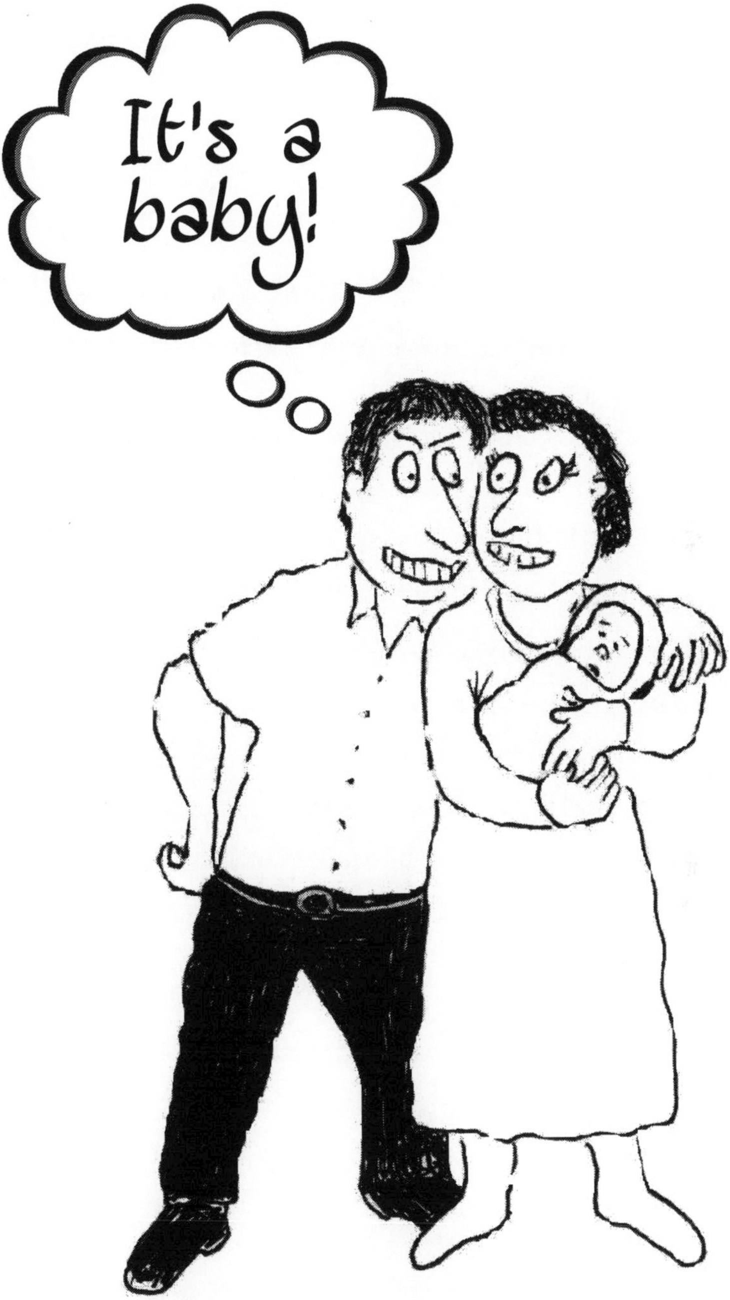
It's a baby!

YOU'RE NOT SUPPOSED TO PULL THEIR LEGS OFF!

On attending his first cardiac arrest, a rookie trainee was trying to remember all he had been taught at training school. On arrival at the scene, the woman was found lying on a bed, without a pulse and not breathing.

The ambulance crew could not carry out effective CPR on the soft bed, so a decision was made to move her off the bed and on to a hard floor. One crew member grabbed the lady' arms as his rookie mate held her ankles. They agreed, on the count of three, to hoist the patient off the bed and place her on the floor.

'One two three LIFT' instructed the crewmate at the head end.

The expression on the rookie's face as the patient's artificial left leg came off in his hand was a sight for sore eyes, and was nowhere to be found in his protocol book!

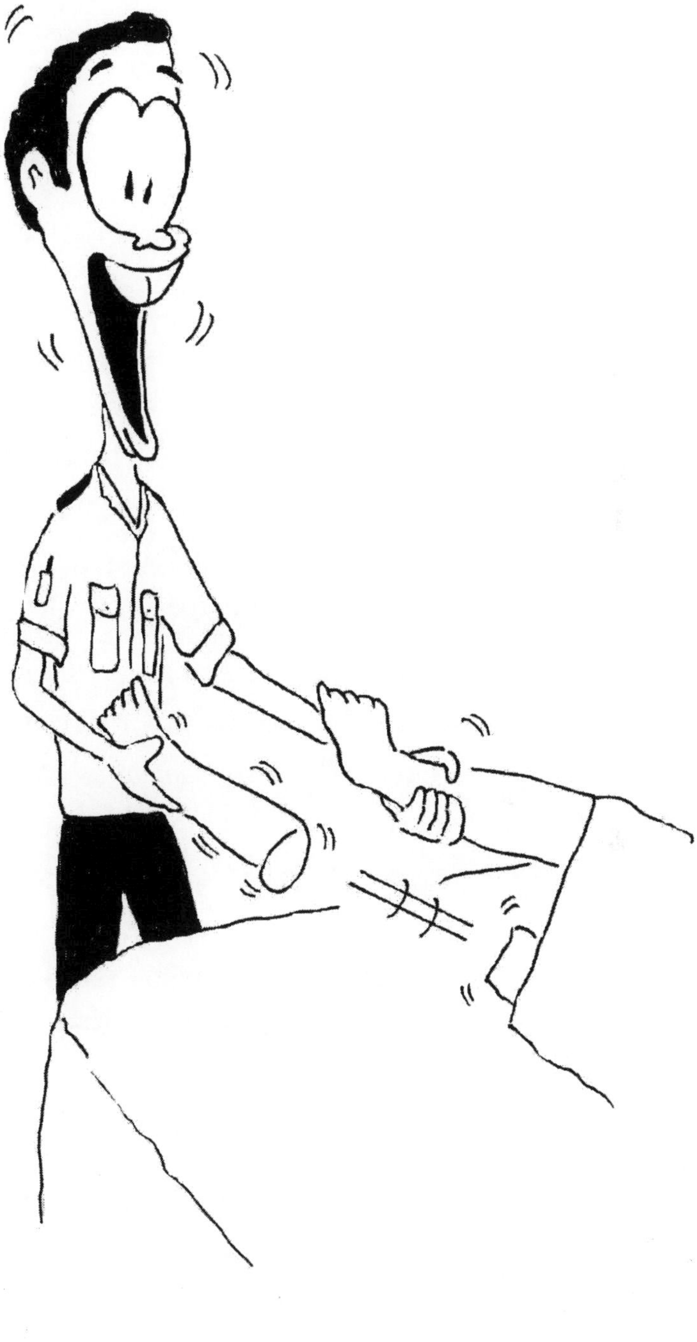

TOILET IN USE

A woman who was suffering from senile dementia managed to ring 999 to call for help. She said her husband had been in the toilet for some time and hadn't drunk his tea.

On arrival, the ambulance crew managed to prize the door open to reveal a man sitting on a toilet, not only dead but in the early stages of rigor mortis. The crew tried to tell the woman that her husband had passed away, but because of her dementia she failed to grasp the situation and started to make her husband a fresh cup of tea.

The crew tried to arrange a doctor's visit for the certification of the body, but was told the doctor couldn't visit for two hours. One of the crew now desperately needed to use the facilities, but the wife told him there was only one loo, although she said he was more than welcome to use it after her husband had finished. Our man had to cross his legs for two hours, and as the only toilet was occupied he asked his crewmate to assist him in making one last examination of the body. They both rocked the corpse until it was in an upright position and would stand up by itself.

'What do you need to check?' said his mate. 'Er, nothing' said the other man, making use of the toilet at last.

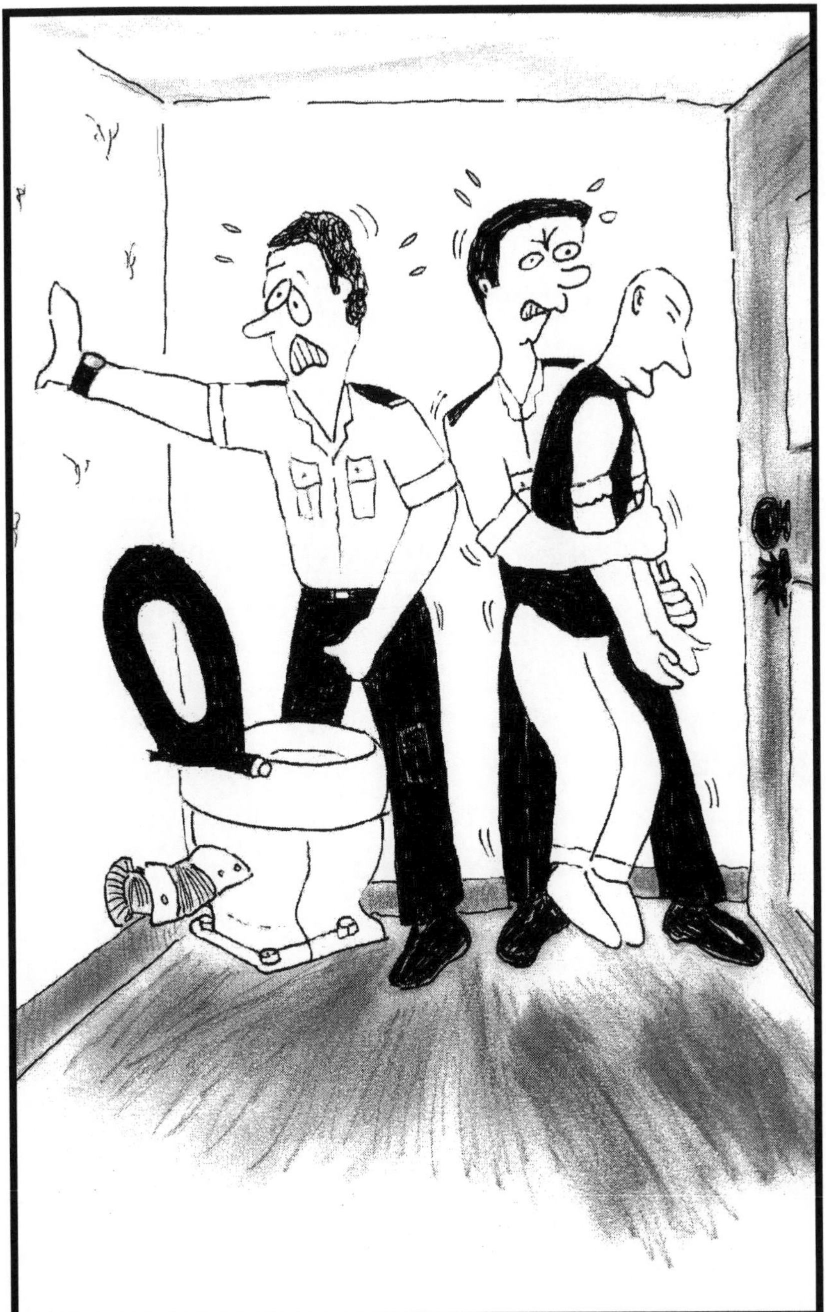

THE PINOCCHIO TREATMENT

With the help of the fire service, a large patient was lifted out of an upstairs bedroom by taking the window out and lifting him on to a bariatric ambulance. Before the journey to hospital commenced, the paramedic placed the patient on oxygen via a nasal cannula.

The fire service followed the ambulance to hospital and on arrival, they hurriedly opened the back doors and started to lift the stretcher out of the vehicle. Unfortunately, the patient was still attached to the nasal cannula, and although the quietly-spoken paramedic tried to alert the firemen to stop, the patient's nose was stretched a good four inches before the oxygen pipe snapped from the flow meter like a whip, saving the patient from having to have a nose transplant!

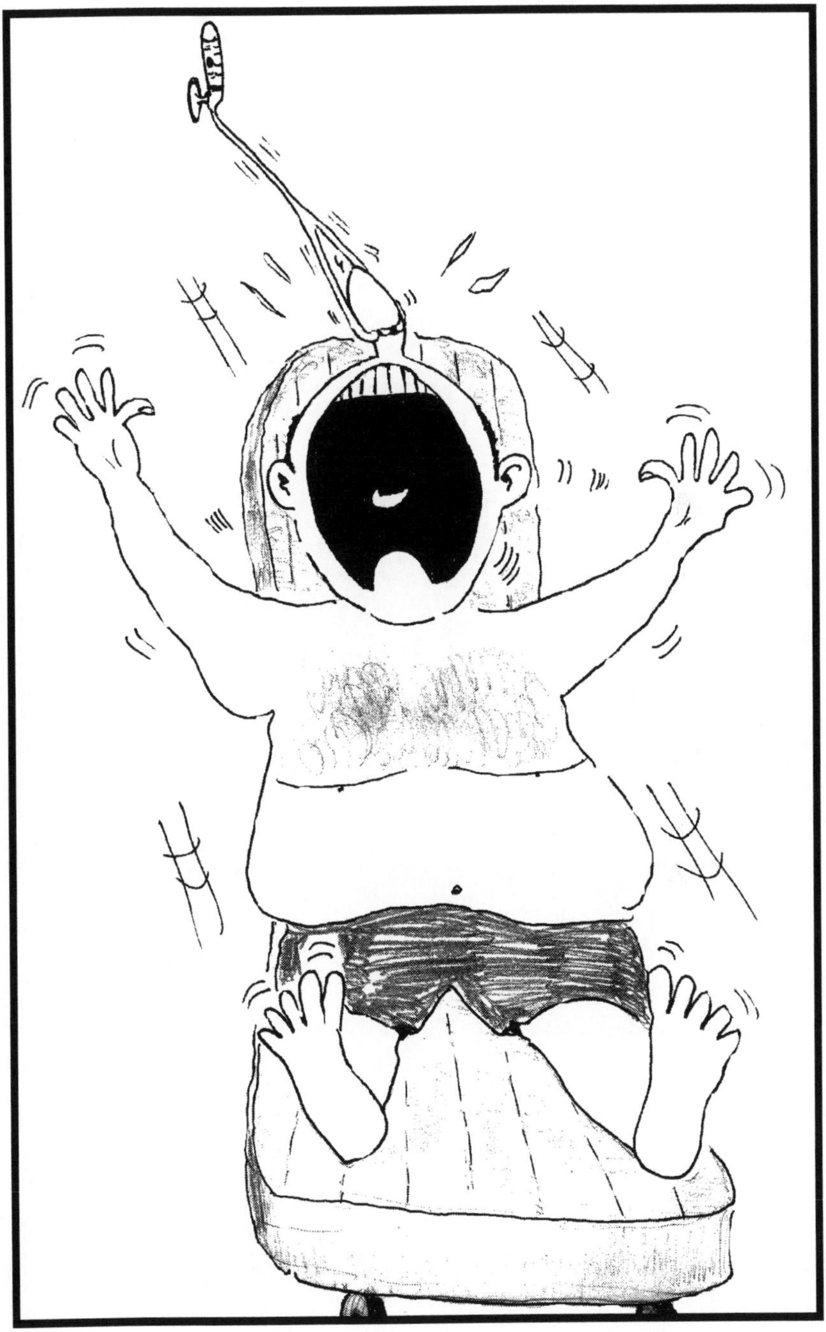

BELLY LAUGH

A female patient had sustained a back injury upstairs in a bedroom. It was essential not to cause her further injury, so the only way she could be brought downstairs was to lie her flat. A scoop stretcher was used, and the crew simultaneously lifted both ends of the scoop and started their difficult descent.

As they were going down the stairs, the patient shouted 'Get that pillow off me, get it off me now!' No pillow had been used on the lift. She was referring to the ambulance man's enormous beer belly, now hanging over her face!

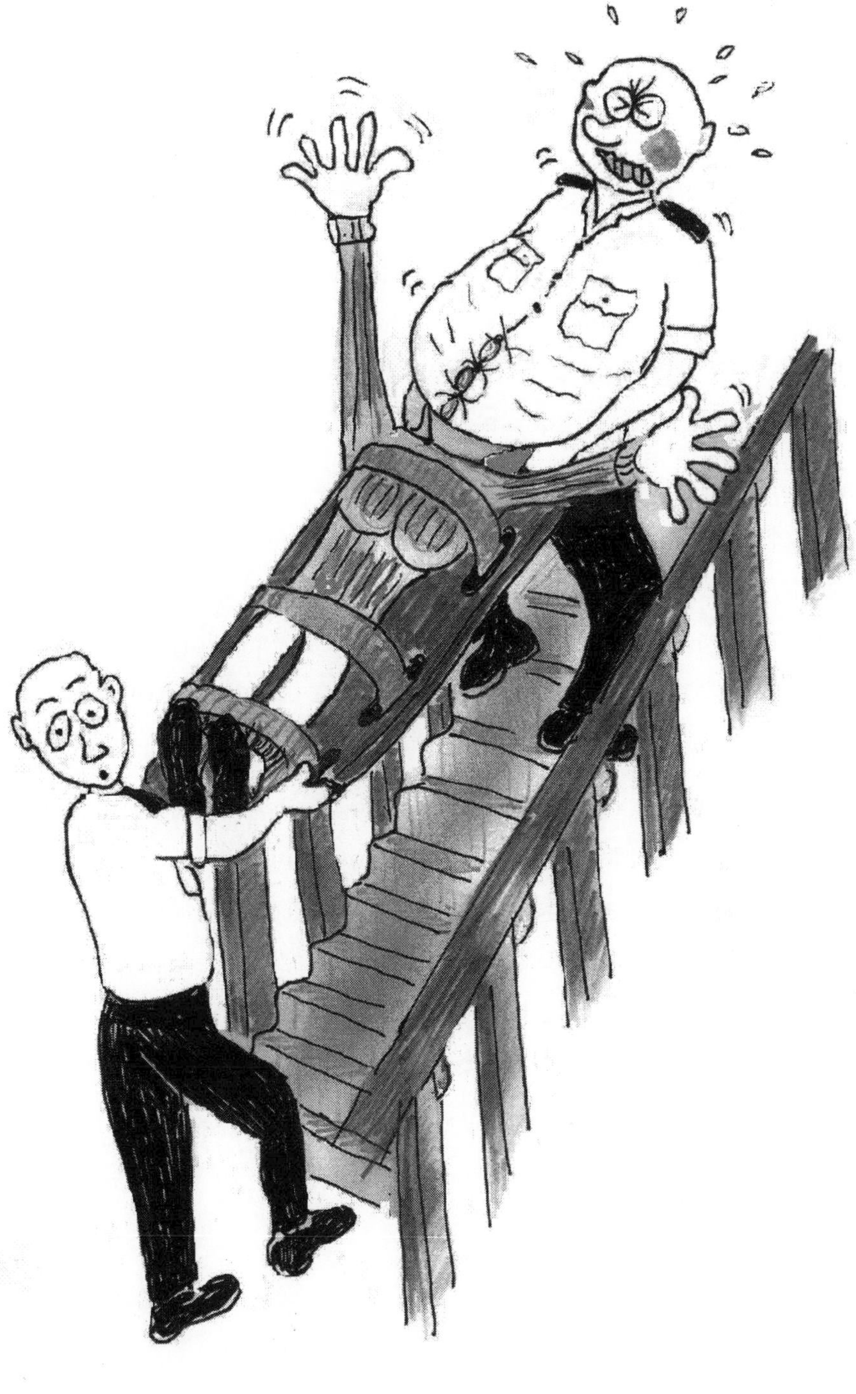

NO SMOKE WITHOUT FIRE

The ambulance service has always had to deal with 'regular callers', people who ring 999 simply because they want to seek attention. Some of these regulars have been known to ring for an ambulance several times in one day, and in those times they would always get a response.

One of these callers was a woman who would regularly call to explain that she had numbness in her breasts and vagina. At 50 years of age, she would attempt to squeeze her nipples to produce droplets of breast milk as evidence to the crew of her loss of sensation.

On this particular occasion, she dialled treble nine to say she had no feeling in her right foot. On arrival of the ambulance, she was accompanied as usual by her 30-year-old son, commonly known to ambulance crews as 'GCS 3'. As the crew were finding out the details of the patient's latest crisis, GCS 3 held a lighter under his mum's foot. She screamed and jumped in the air.

GCS 3 didn't know he had caught his mum out. He thought he had found a miracle cure for his mum's loss of sensation in her foot!

PLEASE RELEASE ME, LET ME GO...

On arrival at the nursing home, the female ambulance crew were directed by nursing staff to a bathroom, where they observed an elderly man sitting in a chair, naked and with only a vanity towel draped across his waist and nether regions. He had obviously had his bath and had been hoisted on to a plastic garden-type chair to be dried off.

The chair had a number of slats in the base, where the patient's bottom had been positioned, but after a little fidgeting both his testicles slipped between two of the slats and dangled beneath the chairs under carriage.

By the time the ambulance crew arrived the plastic seat had somewhat cooled down, but unfortunately the said testicles were now firmly trapped below the base of the chair. Both crew members attempted to relieve the patient's embarrassment by applying copious amounts of hot water, soap and KY Jelly, but to no avail.

Although the predicament was embarrassing for all concerned, the patient managed to see the funny side of a bad situation and started singing that well-known Engelbert Humperdinck song *Please Release Me*.

Unfortunately they couldn't released him, so he was precariously lifted on to a stretcher and carted off to hospital, for further assistance, still singing at the top of his voice.

NO POINT IN GOING HOME

Health service workers generally have a very dark sense of humour, clearly demonstrated at an ex-ambulance man's funeral. Such sad events are among the few gatherings where past and present colleagues meet.

On this particular occasion, colleagues young and old were enjoying each other's company, recalling days gone by. After they had paid their respects at the crematorium, a group of ex-colleagues with an average age of 80 started comparing illnesses and ailments in the garden of remembrance. They were trying to outbid each other on how ill they were, until one old boy said to his retired crewmate, 'Bloody 'ell Bert, you've got so much wrong with you, it's hardly worth going home.'

To an uproar of laughter from his mates!

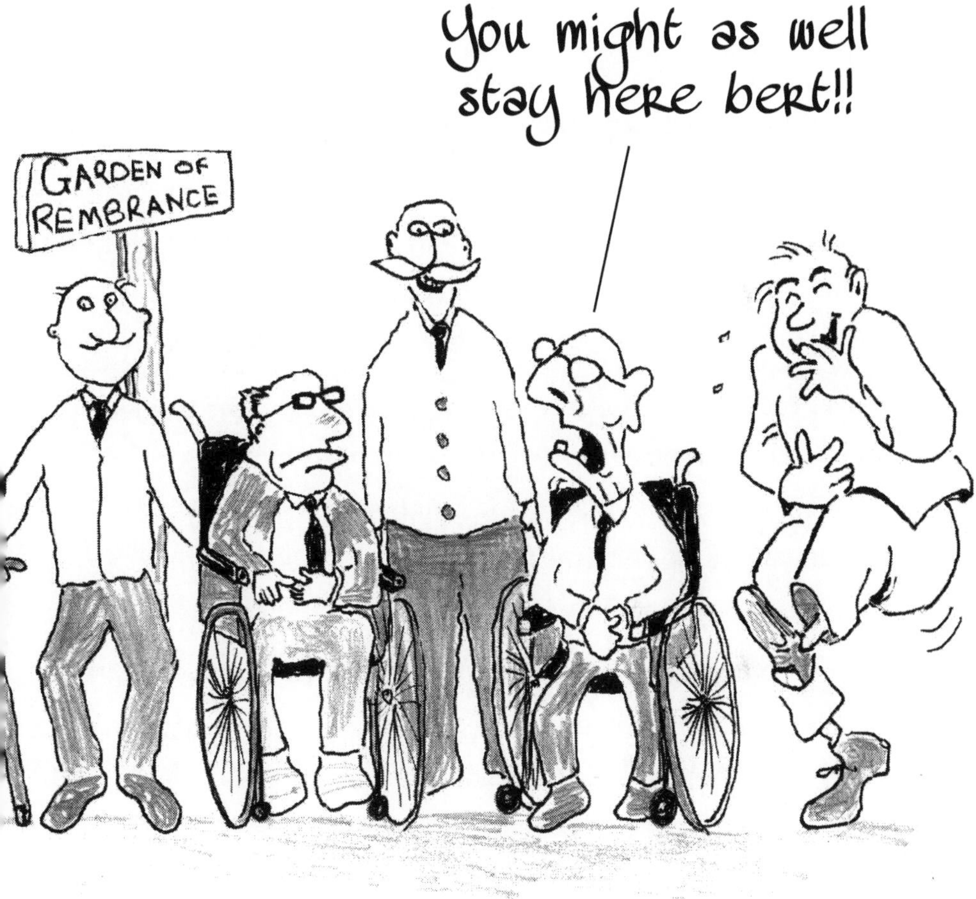
You might as well stay here bert!!
GARDEN OF REMBRANCE

EXTERMINATE, EXTERMINATE!

A manic depressive was threatening to commit suicide. The police were first on scene and discovered a man in his 40s holding a crossbow aimed directly at his own forehead.

The police tried to talk the patient out of pulling the trigger, but it was all to no avail. With the weapon six inches from his head, he pulled the trigger. The bolt penetrated the skin and he fell backwards on to the floor, fully conscious, with the bolt protruding from the centre of his forehead.

When the ambulance crew turned up, the patient had got up off the floor with the bolt still in situ. The crew asked the patient what had happened. He replied, 'I've turned into a Dalek'.

HOLD ON, I'M COMING

When the ambulance men arrived, the female patient announced that she was 'experiencing abdominal sensations'. From the fact that she was grinning from ear to ear, dancing and rolling around the floor with a look of unbridled pleasure on her face, and a porn video was showing on the TV, it was clear that these sensations were sexual in nature.

She admitted to having used a bottle of her husband's GTN spray, which she had sprayed on to her intimate areas, increasing the blood flow and enhancing her pleasure. A dildo was vibrating uncontrollably across the floor.

The crew agreed that the woman was experiencing multiple orgasms. They had no idea what to do with her, given that they were on duty, so they eventually positioned her on all fours on a stretcher and whisked her off to hospital suffering from exhaustion, still howling and shouting, 'Yes, yes, yes!' every thirty seconds.

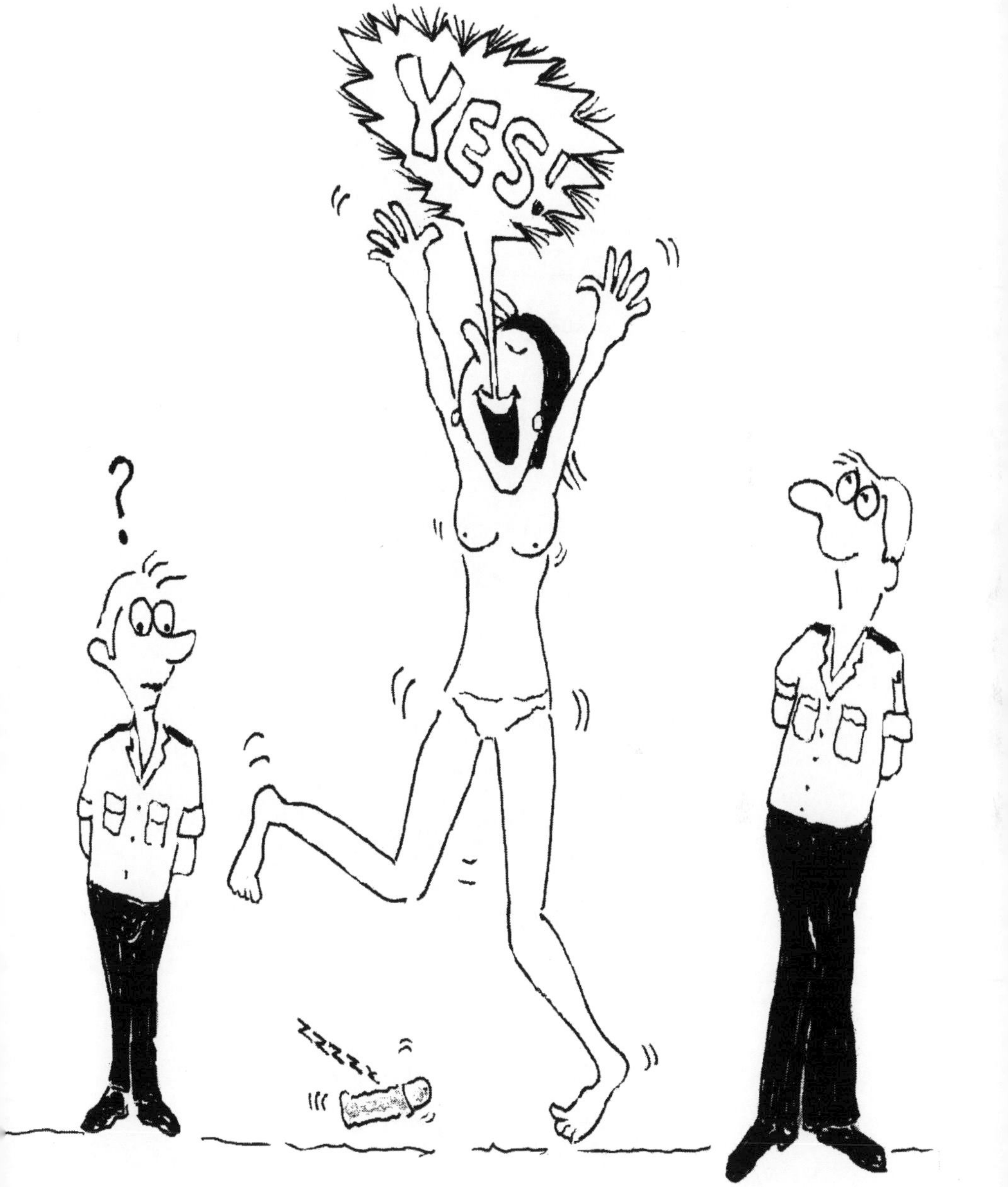
YES!
?
ZZZZZ

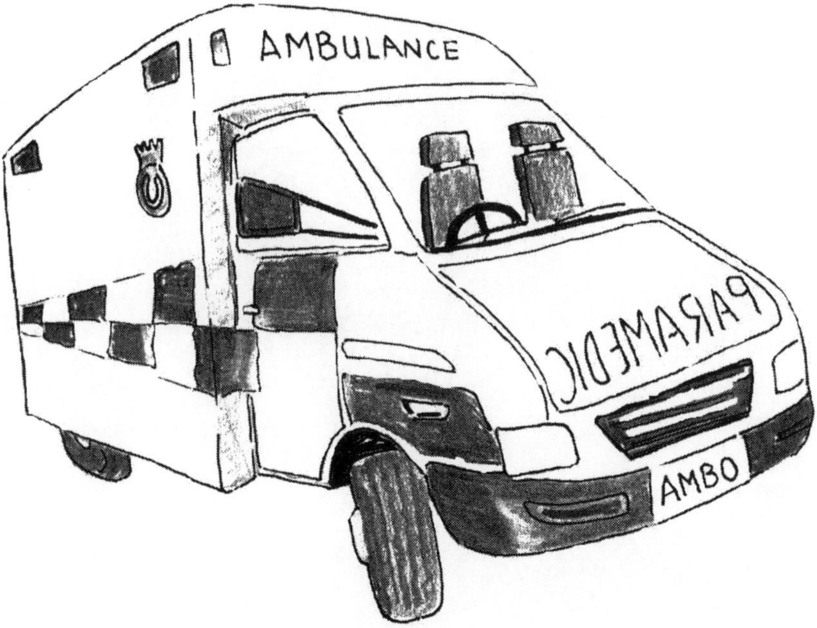
AMBULANCE
AMBO

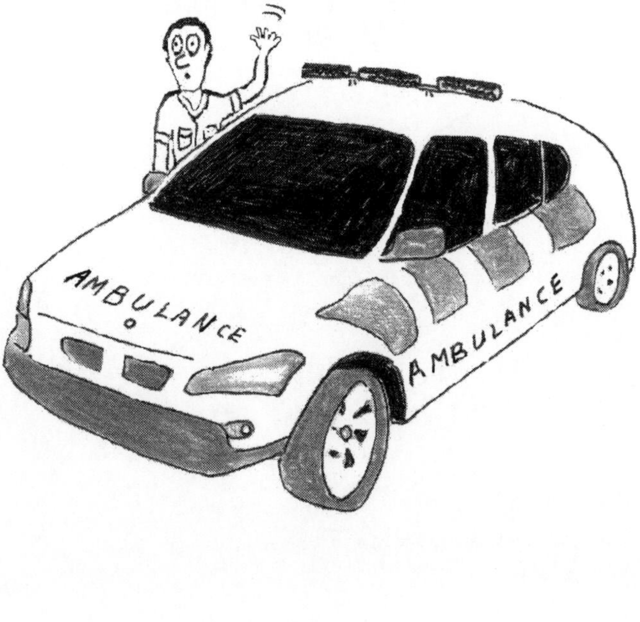
AMBULANCE
AMBULANCE

2000 AND BEYOND

WEIGHTY DECISION

DOWN, BOY!

THE WRONG LANGUAGE

YOU'RE NEVER TOO OLD...

WRONG END OF THE STICK

FIVE MINUTES OUT OF DATE

OH, AND BY THE WAY...

GETTING THE MESSAGE

ONE WAY TO STOP A DRUNK DRIVER

WRONG KIND OF COMA

OOPS, WRONG BALLS!

LEFT IN THE LURCH

SHORT CUT TO DISASTER

INDECENT ASSAULT

KISSES SWEETER THAN WINE

THE MOUNTAIN COMES TO MOHAMED

OPTICAL ILLUSION

LOVE WILL KEEP US TOGETHER

HERE, KITTY KITTY

KNICKERS IN A TWIST

EMERGENCY, MY TV REMOTE IS DEAD

WEIGHTY DECISION

Sometimes paramedics get sent out on the strangest emergency calls. One of the oddest was when a concerned resident rang 999 because he thought his neighbour was becoming dangerously overweight.

On arrival, the crew first had to explain to the patient why they had been called and second, they had to explain to the concerned resident why they couldn't just drag his neighbour off to hospital and put him on a diet!

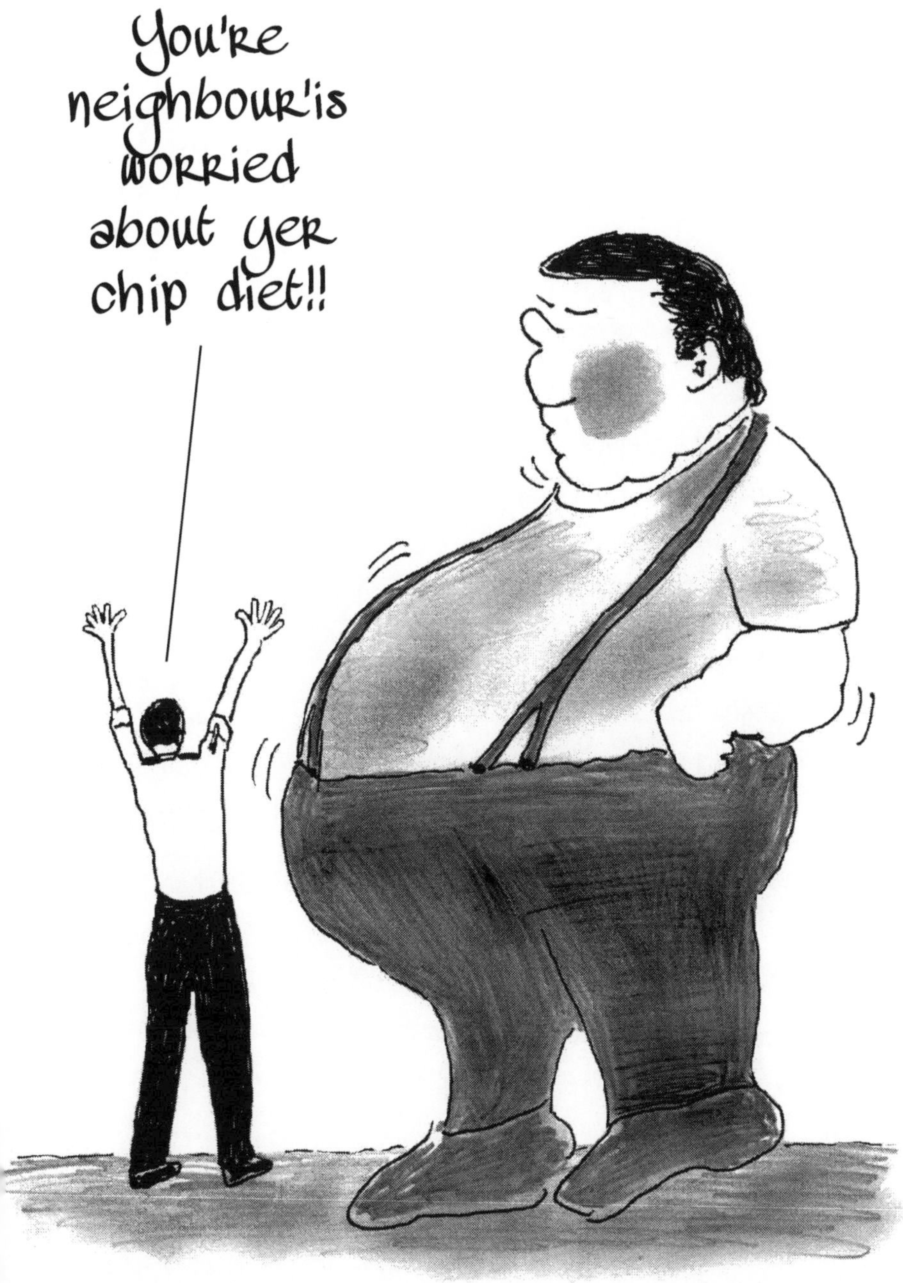
You're neighbour'is worried about yer chip diet!!

DOWN, BOY!

An ambulance crew were performing CPR. in a desperate attempt to resuscitate a man who had collapsed. They were about to administer a shot of adrenaline when the paramedic's crewmate said 'Stop, I can feel a pulse!'

Adrenaline was contraindicated, which disturbed the paramedics' protocol. 'What shall I do with this adrenaline I've drawn up?' said the paramedic. In the absence of a repeatable reply, he decided to squirt the contents into the dog's bowl.

On seeing the arrival of this unexpected treat Fido rushed straight to the bowl and lapped up the contents. For the next 10 minutes he could do nothing but run around in circles.

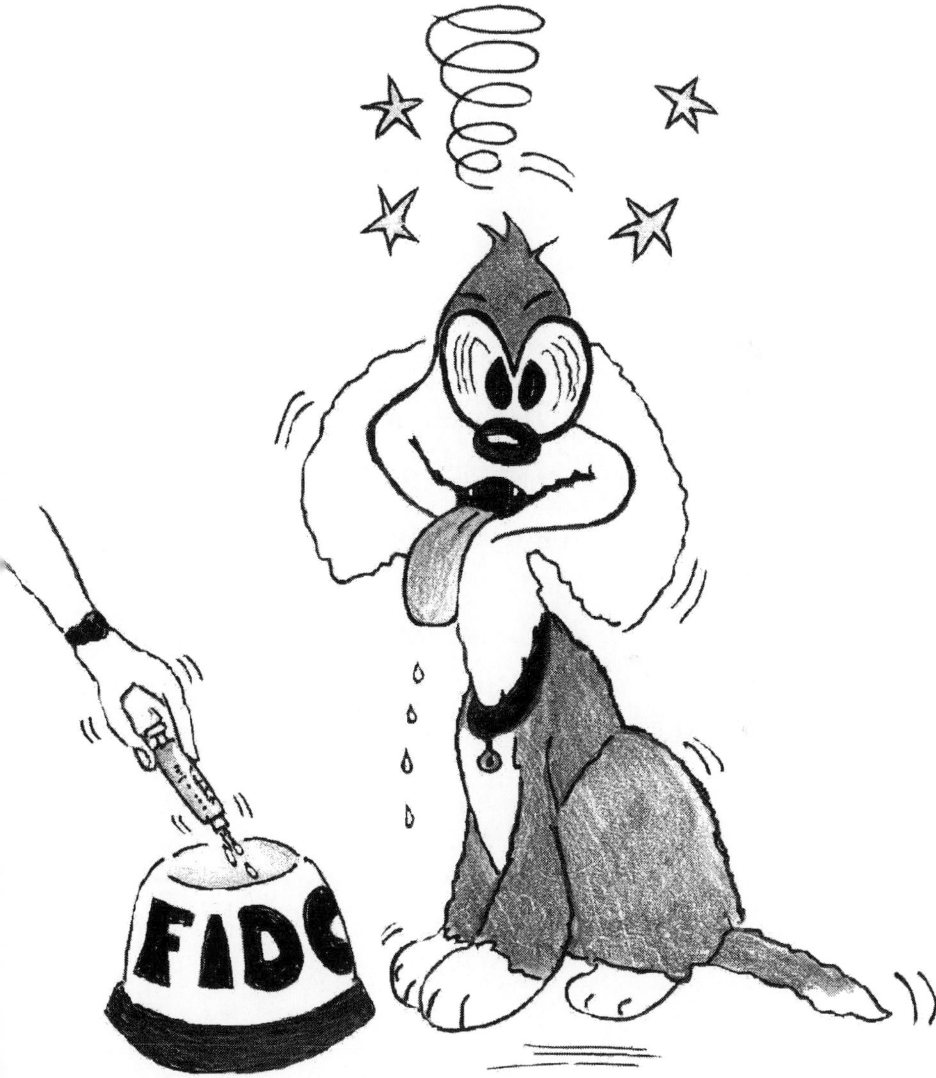
FIDO

THE WRONG LANGUAGE

Having responded to a call to see a patient who was 'refusing to co-operate', the ambulance crew arrived at a house where the occupants were Polish. The patient was refusing to communicate with anyone.

With the assistance of the other Polish housemates, the crew tried to establish what was wrong with the man, but he continued to stay silent and uncooperative. The ambulance service even arranged for a Polish interpreter to talk through any medical matters with the patient on the phone, but the patient remained silent with a blank expression on his face.

At last, in sheer frustration, he stood up and shouted out, 'I am RUSSIAN!'

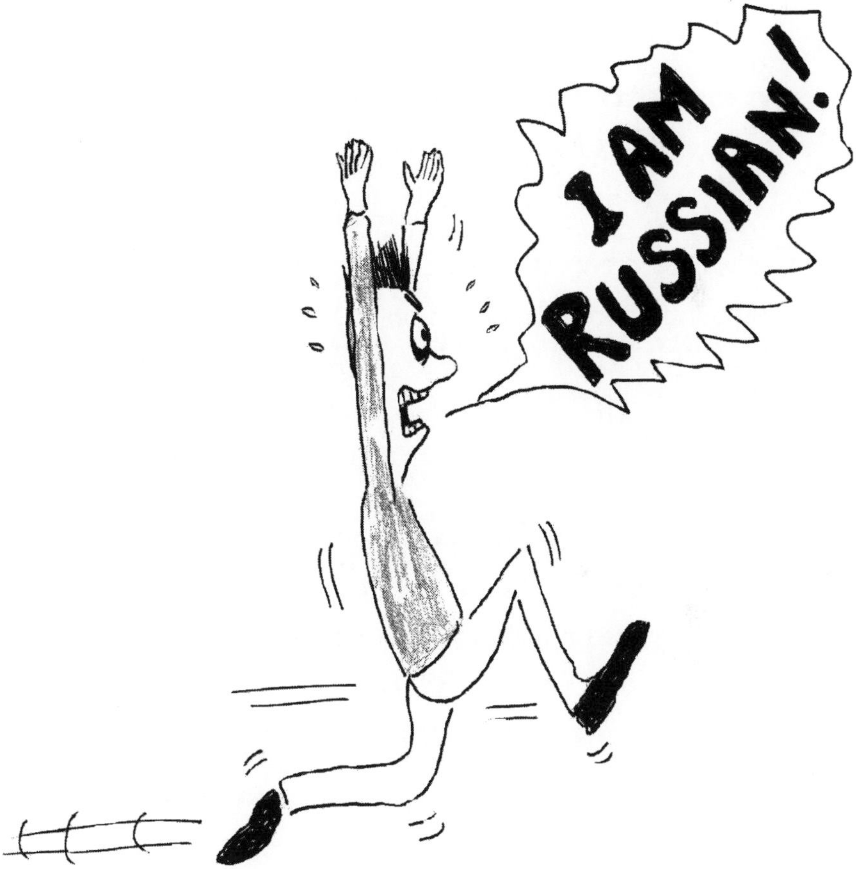
I AM RUSSIAN!

YOU'RE NEVER TOO OLD...

An ambulance crew was called to a man who had been discharged after suffering a stroke. His wife had called for the ambulance, saying her husband was 'not quite his normal self'.

On arrival, the crew was directed into a bedroom to find a frail elderly gentleman lying in bed bolt upright, gripping the bed sheets with his teeth. The crew asked what was wrong with her husband. The wife said, 'Since he's come out of hospital after his stroke, he's continually masturbating.'

The crew was in shock as his wife continued, 'He's at it all the time, in the bedroom and the bathroom. The home help is at her wits' end, she's having to change the sheets daily. I think it's since they've changed his medication.'

One of the crew said, 'What's he on now, Viagra?' On hearing this, his crewmate had to leave the room for fear of bursting out in uncontrolled laughter.

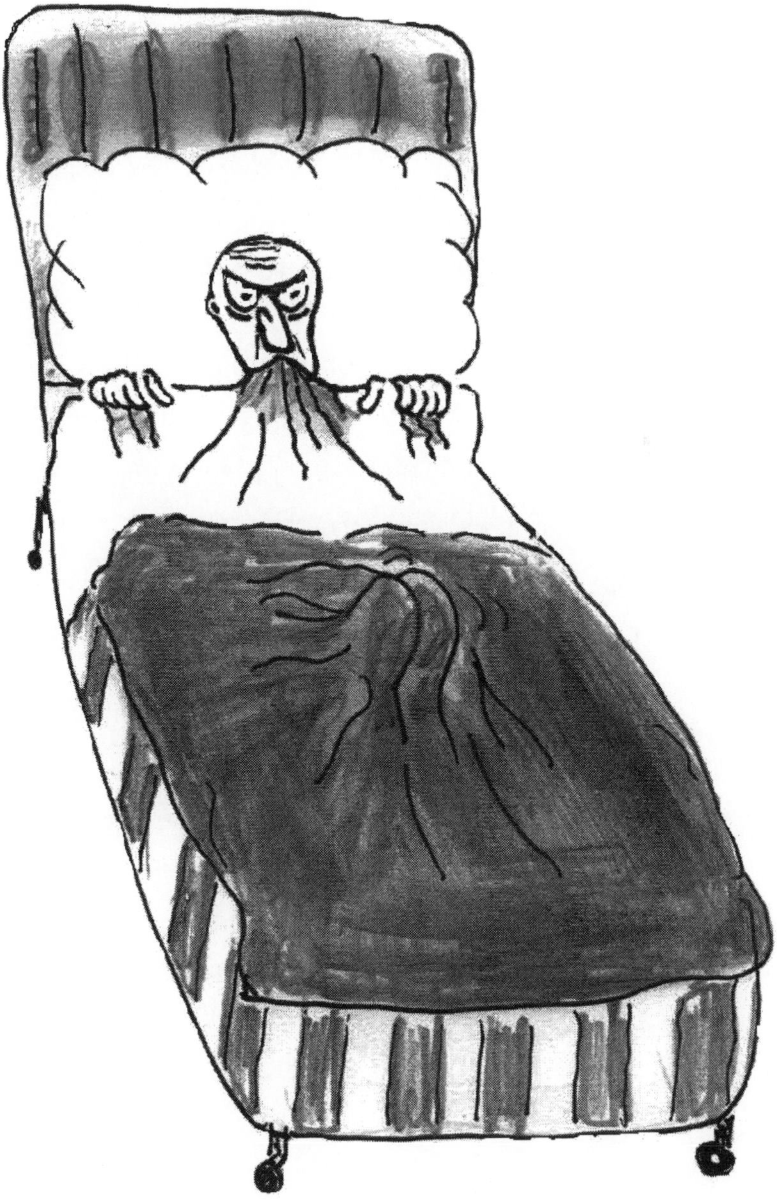

WRONG END OF THE STICK

A patient was admitted by ambulance to the A&E department with breathing difficulties. After he had been assessed, the doctor prescribed the medication aminophiline, in the form of rectal suppositories.

The staff nurse gave the student nurse the two suppositories. The student asked her what they were for.

"They're for the patient's breathing" she said.

Off went the student nurse with the two suppositories. When she was checked by the staff nurse 10 minutes later, she found the patient with the suppositories stuck up his nostrils.

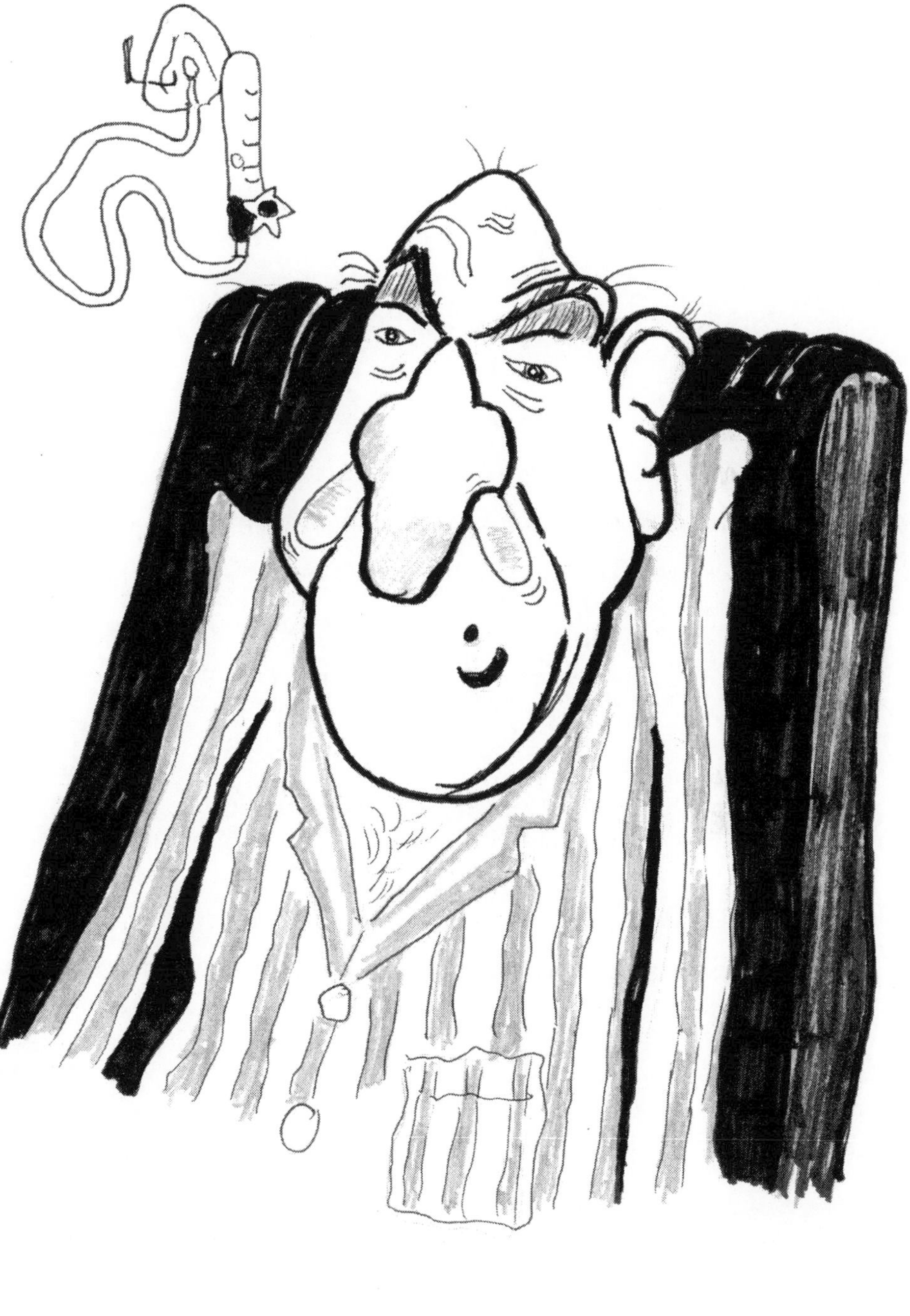

FIVE MINUTES OUT OF DATE

It was five minutes past midnight on the third of the month when an ambulance crew responded to a reported case of food poisoning. The paramedic was met at the door by a very nervous male, who directed him to his fridge. He showed him a block of cheese which had gone out of date on the 2nd of the month. The patient had phoned 999 to see if his cheese was still safe to eat.

The paramedic said his cheese did look OK, but advised him to make a ham sandwich instead because the cheese would probably give him nightmares.

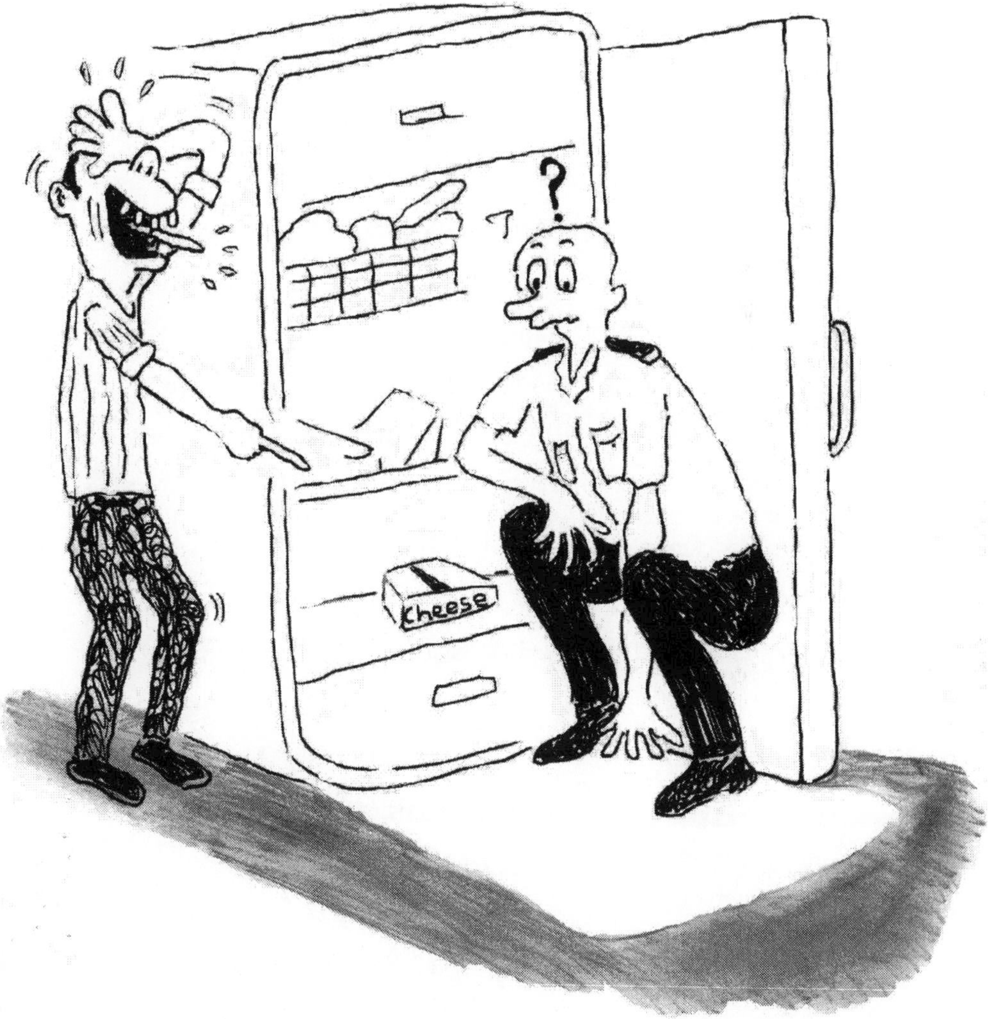
Cheese

OH, AND BY THE WAY...

A responder was assigned to a call which was described as a male with 'shortage of breath'. The paramedic was wondering what type of medical emergency he could be attending – a heart attack or asthma attack, perhaps. He thought he had mentally prepared himself for the kind of call he would probably be dealing with, until the patient's wife led him down the garden path and into a garage.

Here he discovered that her husband's car jack had partially collapsed while he was changing a tyre, resulting in the vehicle pressing down on hubby's chest, causing, understandably, a 'shortage of breath'. She had forgotten to mention the slightly more obvious point that a car had collapsed on to the poor bloke.

GETTING THE MESSAGE

A paramedic responder attended an obviously-deceased patient. After filling out all the paperwork, it was time to break the sad news to the deceased patient's relatives that their loved one had indeed passed on to a better place.

As he left the bedroom and was entering the room where the relatives had gathered, he received a text. Too late, he realised that his new text message alert, the song "Welcome to the dark side, welcome to hell", was somewhat inappropriate.

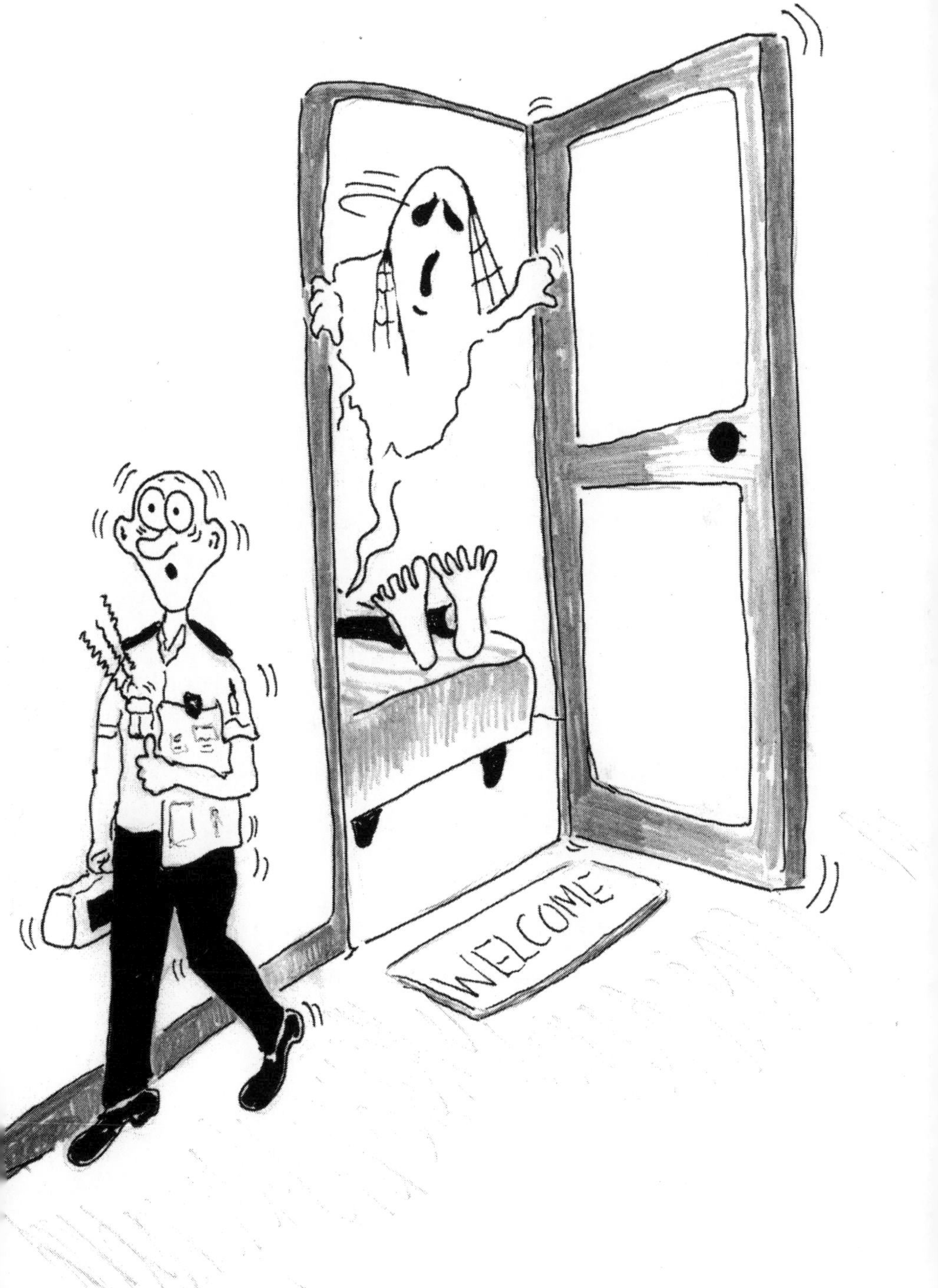
WELCOME

ONE WAY TO STOP A DRUNK DRIVER

A night out ended in tears for one young woman, thanks to her boyfriend's drinking. The man insisted he was going to drive home, much to the annoyance of his girl, who knew he was way over the drink-drive limit.

She tried in vain to get hold of his car keys, but the boyfriend held on to them and managed to open the driver's door. In a drastic last-ditch attempt to stop him driving, the woman pushed her boyfriend out of the way and managed to squeeze her head beneath the steering wheel and get stuck, stopping him from driving.

The fire brigade had to cut through the steering wheel before she was boarded and collared and taken to hospital.

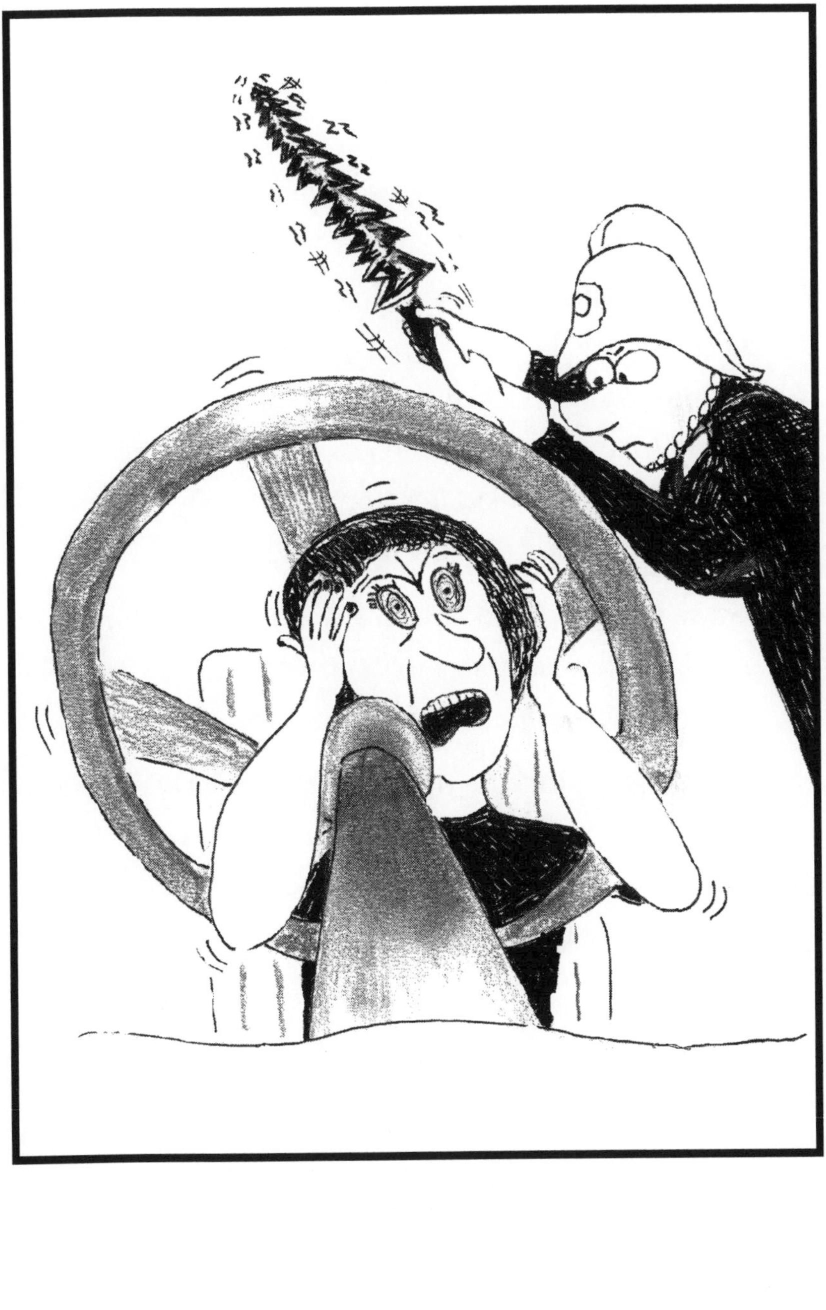

WRONG KIND OF COMA

A report of a diabetic experiencing a hypoglycaemic episode could easily be dealt with, thought the paramedic solo responder as he knocked on the door of a non-English-speaking Asian household. He was met by a young Asian boy, who led him to a male in a front room, lying on a settee and seemingly unconscious.

It was difficult to communicate with the boy, but observations commenced and the responder used a needle to ascertain the patient's blood sugar level.

It didn't take too long for the paramedic to realise that he was not only treating the wrong patient - he was in the wrong street. Mr Singh was not amused at being woken up so rudely from his night shift!

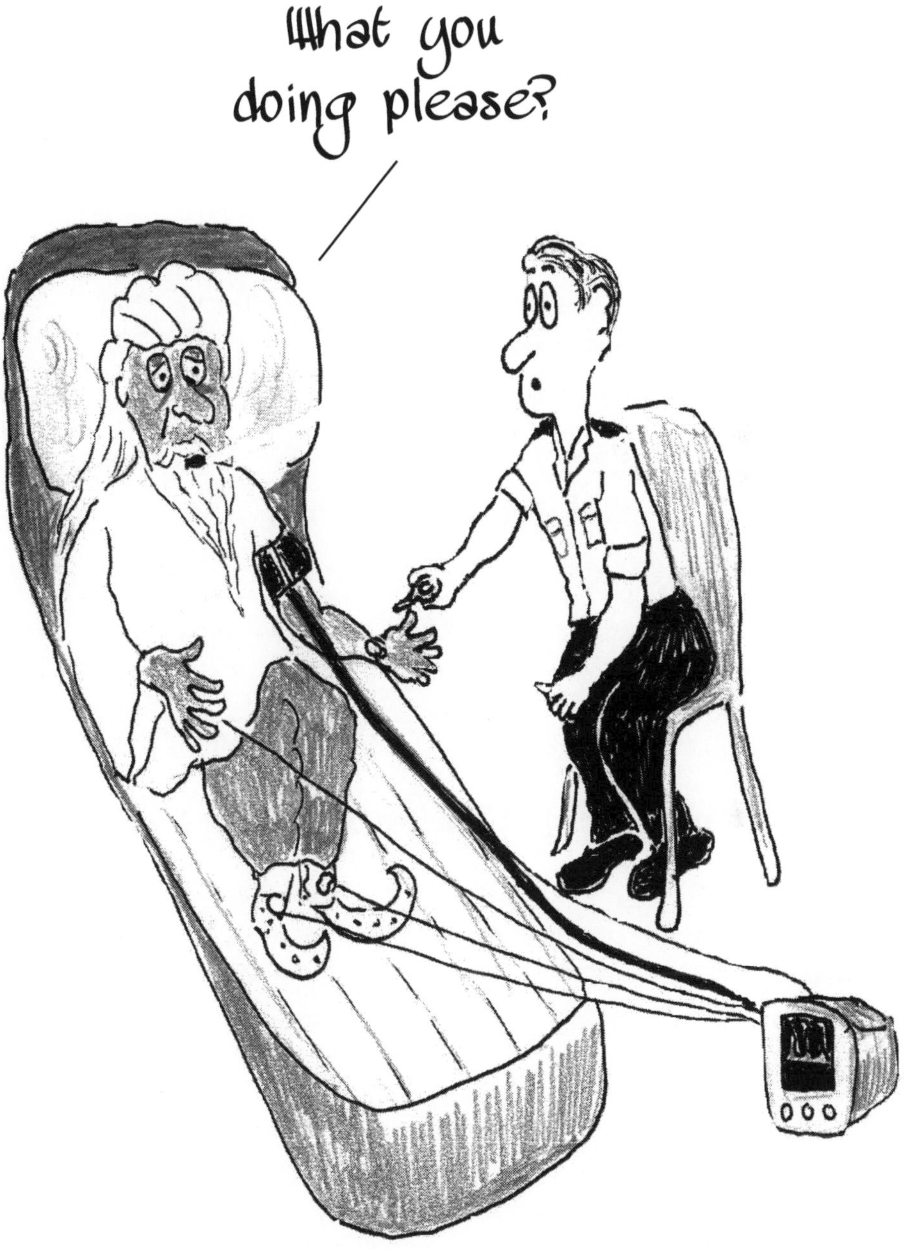
What you doing please?

OOPS, WRONG BALLS!

A crew was called to assist an 84-year-old man suffering from shortness of breath. After observations had been completed, the patient was placed on oxygen and the man was about to be carried out to the waiting ambulance. Unfortunately the patient's wire-haired terrier had taken an instant dislike to the ambulance crew, who appeared to be kidnapping his owner.

The patient's wife could see the potential for conflict as the dog continued snarling at the crew. 'If the dog gives you any problems, just kick his balls, that should do the trick' she said. The ambulance crew looked at each other, somewhat dismayed, and tried to get to the front door, much to the displeasure of the dog, who started biting their ankles.

Following the wife's instructions, one of the crew kicked the dog clean between the legs. It yelped and flew through the air. The wife was furious. 'I meant the footballs in his basket!' she stormed.

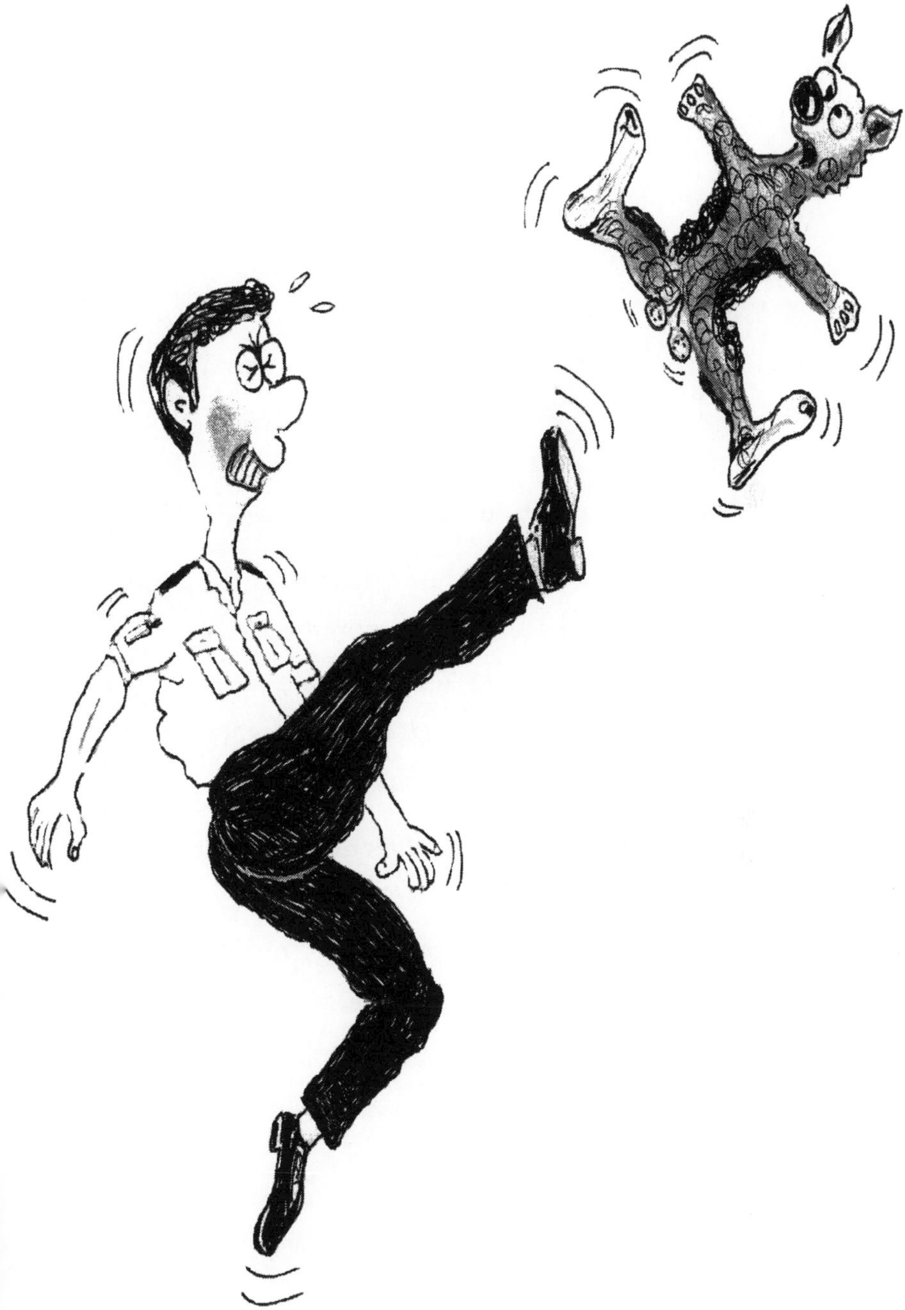

LEFT IN THE LURCH

Having picked up a patient who had taken an overdose, an ambulance driver had to perform a difficult manoeuvre to get out of the cul-de-sac. The attendant jumped out of the ambulance to help guide the vehicle back.

Having watched and waved back the ambulance, the attendant began to pick up his equipment. 'OK to go?' shouted the driver into the back of the ambulance. 'Yep no problem' the patient replied. The driver took his word for it and accelerated away - leaving his crewmate and equipment at the scene.

It was only when the ambulance driver got to hospital and opened the back doors that he realised he had not only left the patient unattended for the journey but had left his crewmate at the house.

SHORT CUT TO DISASTER

A three-man crew arrived at sheltered accommodation in the early hours to attend to a 90-year-old woman who had suffered a fall. But the warden had the key, and he was still a car ride away.

The ambulance men spotted a small window open at the rear of the building, which appeared to lead into the toilet block. The junior member of the crew, who happened to be the smallest, volunteered to climb through the window, attend to the patient and wait for the warden to arrive. The other two lifted 'junior' level with the window and dropped him in.

Mistake. He smashed the cistern on entry, and then found that the main toilet door was locked, as the facilities were not used at night. Not only did the crew have to wait for the warden to open both the front door and the communal toilets, he had to call out an emergency plumber to mend the cistern!

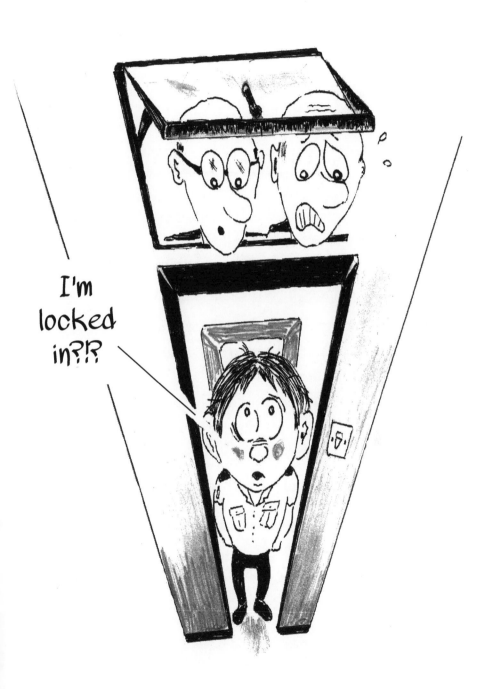

I'm
locked
in?!?

INDECENT ASSAULT

A paramedic was sent to attend a female patient, finding her lying on the floor in the front living room with a badly-fractured arm. She told the attending paramedic that she had tripped on one of her pet's toys.

The paramedic bent down on his hands and knees to further assess the lady and decided to cannulate her to give the patient pain relief. He found an appropriate cannulation site and was just about to puncture the vein when he heard a sniffing noise at his rear end and thought 'hang on a minute, what's going on here?'

He suddenly realised that he was being 'taken' from behind by the family dog.

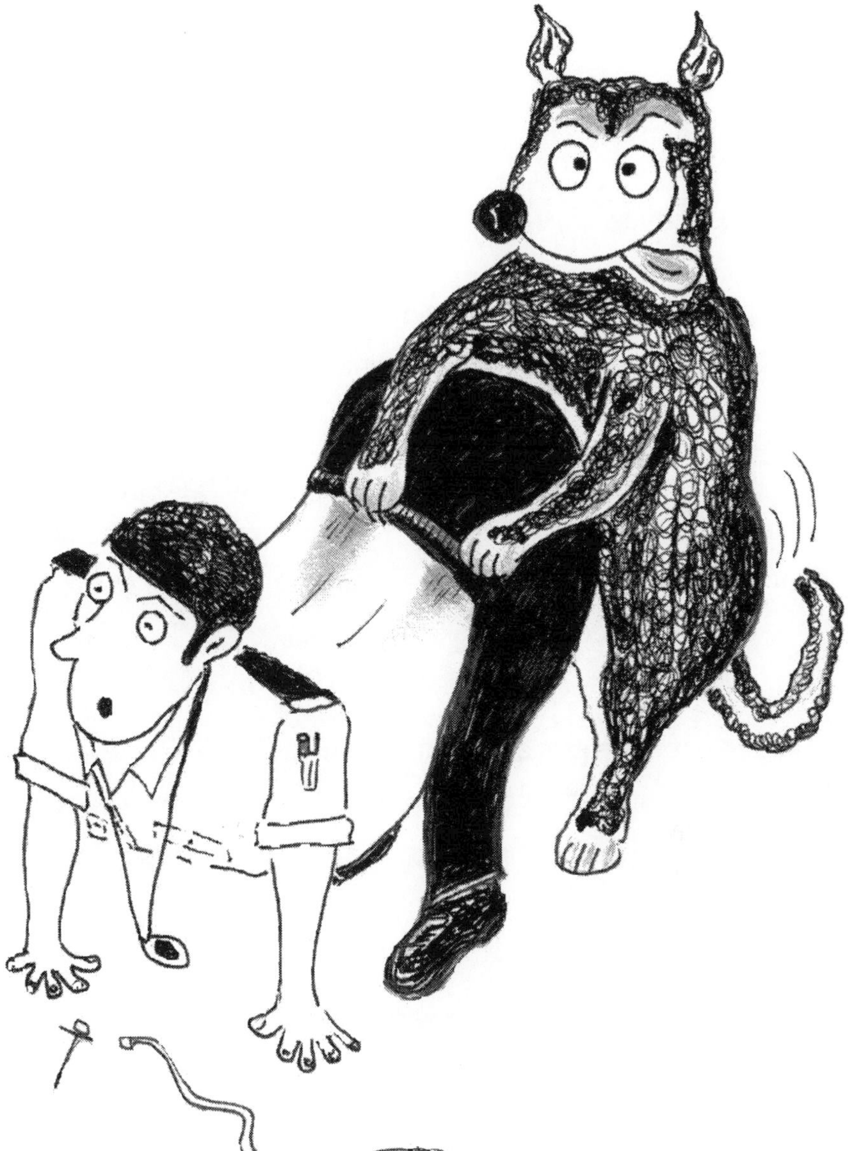
BAXTERS

KISSES SWEETER THAN WINE

An emergency care practitioner was called to assist an ambulance crew with a female patient suffering from abdominal pains. The lady had been vomiting and had a high temperature.

The ambulance crew was aware that the lady was getting married in the morning and was wondering whether she was suffering from anxiety after contracting a urine infection. The practitioner decided to take a urine sample and the lady passed water into a mug provided.

The patient complained that she was feeling sick, and requested water. The paramedic placed the mug of water on the table just as the patient returned with the urine sample in an identical mug. Unfortunately, the patient got the mugs mixed up and drank out of the one containing the urine.

Her main concern after that was the first kiss she would be giving her husband on her wedding day!

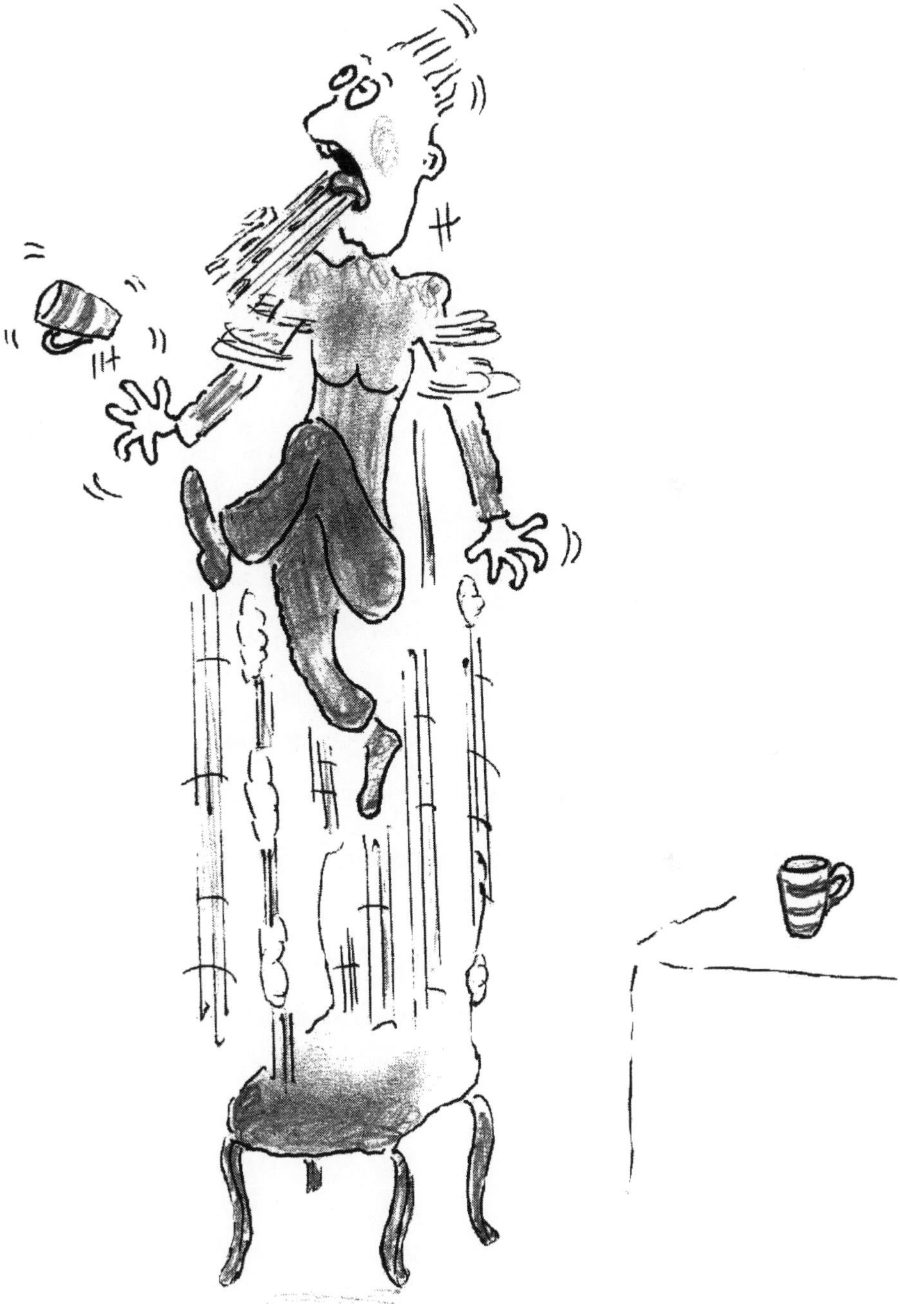

THE MOUNTAIN COMES
TO MOHAMED

When a paramedic responder received a treble-nine call to a collapse case at a railway station, she made good time and arrived on the scene within eight minutes. On arrival she received a further update, learning that the patient was a train driver who had just left the station when he had passed out.

The paramedic could see the train a quarter of a mile down the track, but because of health and safety, she was forbidden to go to the train. The train had to come to her.

Arrangements were made for the train to be pushed back into the railway station. The recorded response times were 'Call time to scene - 8 minutes. At-scene time to patient contact - One hour 15 minutes.'

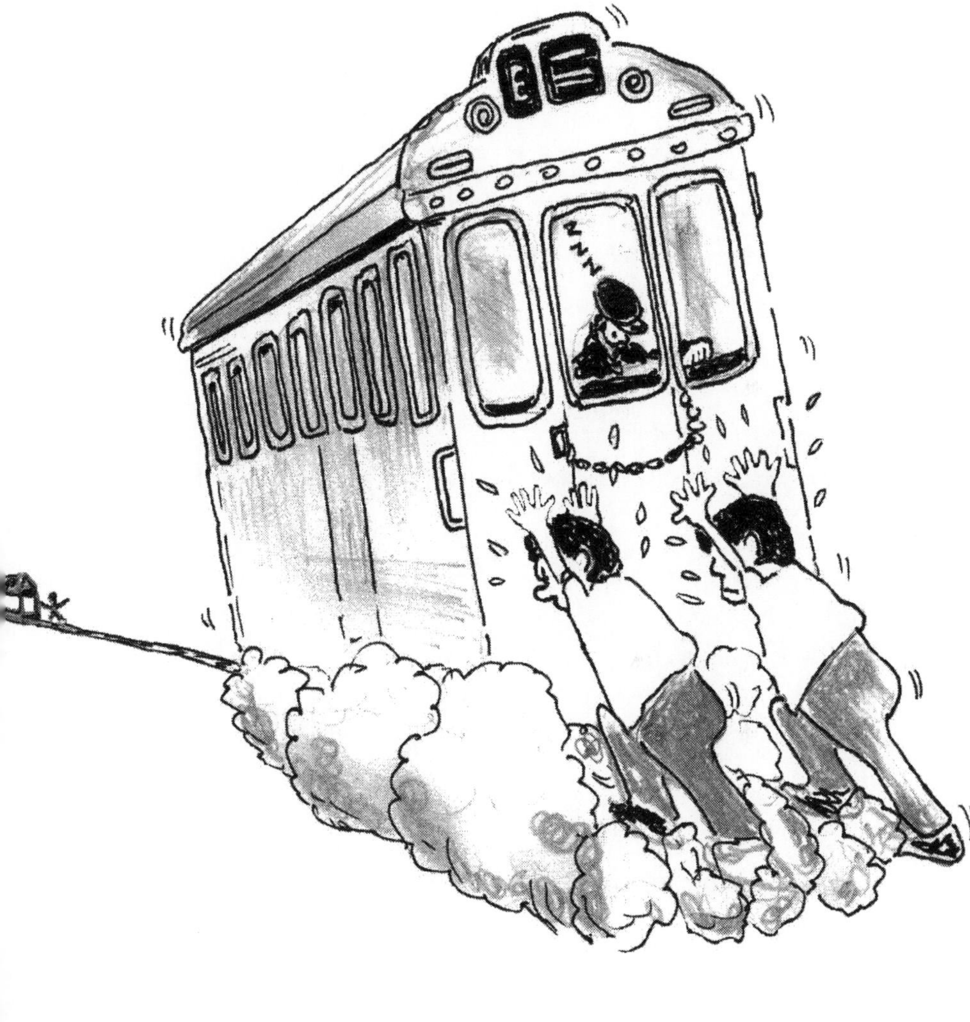

OPTICAL ILLUSION

On a night shift at 3 am, a report of a child of approximately six years of age dangling out of a window would make the most hardened ambulance man's heart race. But that was how the emergency was described.

The crew screeched down the road to arrive at a detached house on the corner of the street. They were flagged down by a middle-aged man who was clearly the worse for wear from a night on the drink.

He slurred, 'There he is!' and pointed to the 'child'. It was a ventilation pipe hanging out of a window, obviously attached to a tumble drier and held flimsily in position by a weight to stop it flapping. Emergency over.

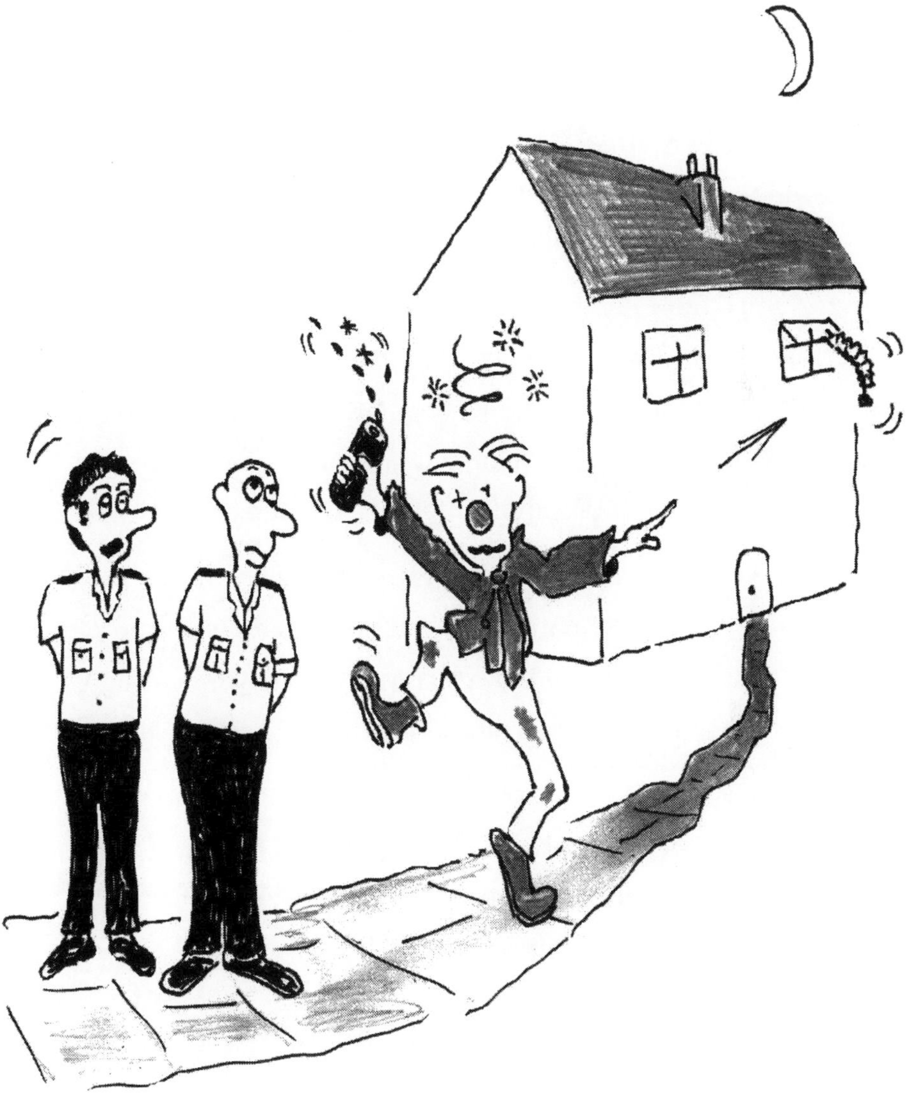

LOVE WILL KEEP US TOGETHER

A crew got a call which was given as 'man and woman trapped.' They had no idea what they were about to find behind closed doors.

The young couple had been together for six months and at the tender age of 17 years they decided to make love for the first time. To help proceedings along, they had decided to use what they thought, was a bottle of lubricant. Unfortunately they had smeared over their bodies the contents of a bottle of superglue.

When the crew arrived, the couple were completely naked and locked together. The man's penis was stuck to his girlfriend's left buttock and his right hand was firmly attached to her thigh. One of the girl's hands was glued to an internal plaster wall.

The crew had to borrow a crowbar from next door to break the plaster from around the wall. They managed to place the unfortunate couple on the same stretcher and conveyed them both to A&E to apply solvent, much to the amusement of the casualty staff.

HERE, KITTY KITTY

There were no two-man ambulances available to attend a call to a cardiac arrest, so two solo paramedic responders dealt with it. On arrival they had difficulty in trying to clear an obstructed airway. The aspirated contents were described by the paramedics as like a conveyor belt of disgorged garlic bread.

At the side of the patient's head on the paramedic's blind side, a chomping noise could be heard. It was the family cat, attempting to chomp away at the discarded residue which had just been removed from the mouth of the patient. The crew asked in no uncertain terms that the animal should be removed from the room while the ambulance staff tried to do their job under such difficult circumstances.

Finally, just as the paramedic had finished working on the patient's airway, the ambulance crew arrived. As the door flew open the ravenous pet re-entered the room and again started chomping on the discarded contents. The paramedic grabbed the cat and in rugby fashion passed it out of the 'scrum' to one of the crew, who then attempted a backward pass into the arms of the wife. She fly-passed it out of the back door, to land perfectly in the cat basket as the door slammed shut.

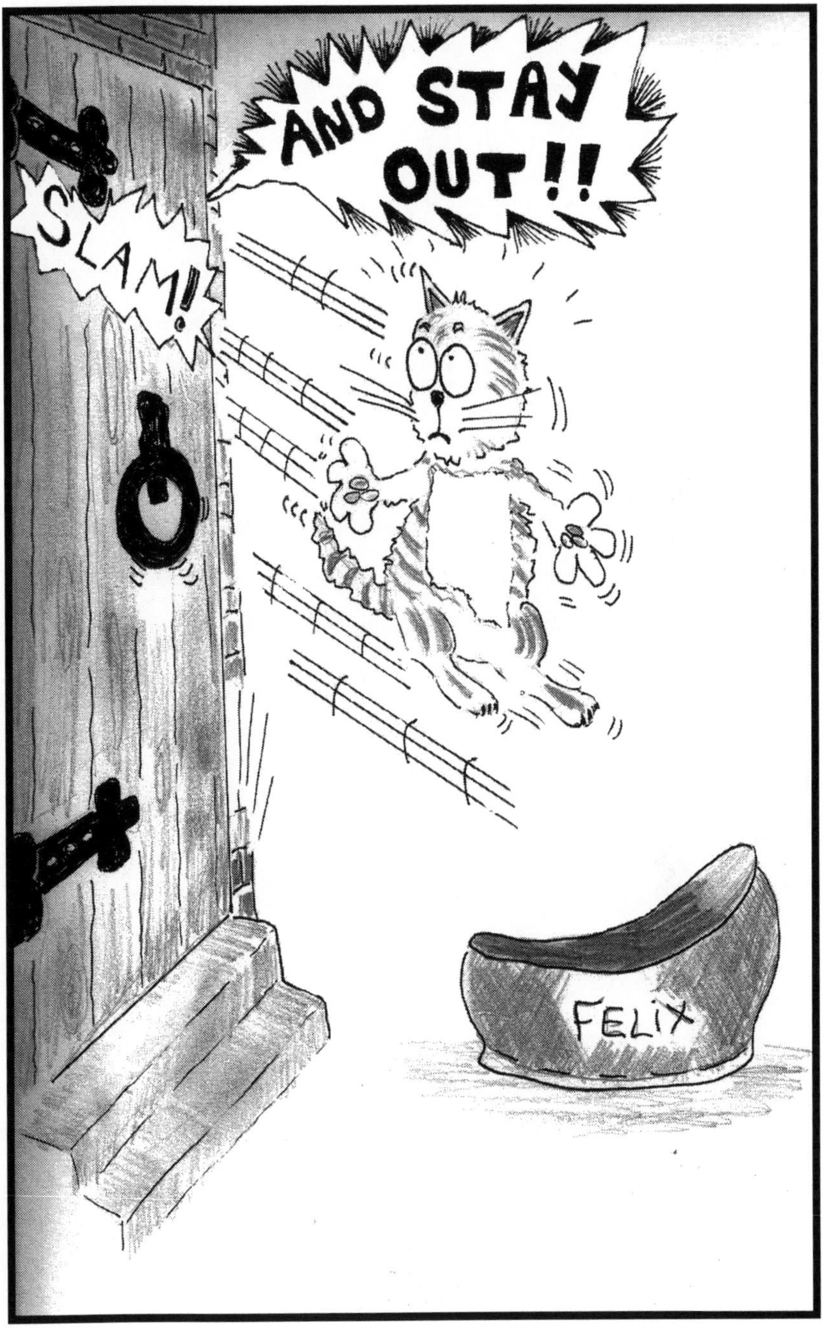
SLAM!!
AND STAY OUT!!
FELIX

KNICKERS IN A TWIST

The crew was called to attend an elderly male at his home address, who was sweating and suffering shortness of breath. They found him naked. After the crew had decided that the patient needed to go to hospital, they explained that he would have to take some clothes with him for when he was eventually discharged.

The crew members ran around like headless chickens trying to find something for him to put on. On exploring both rooms, they had no option but to put him in the only clothes they could find - a polka-dot dress and a pair of ladies' knickers.

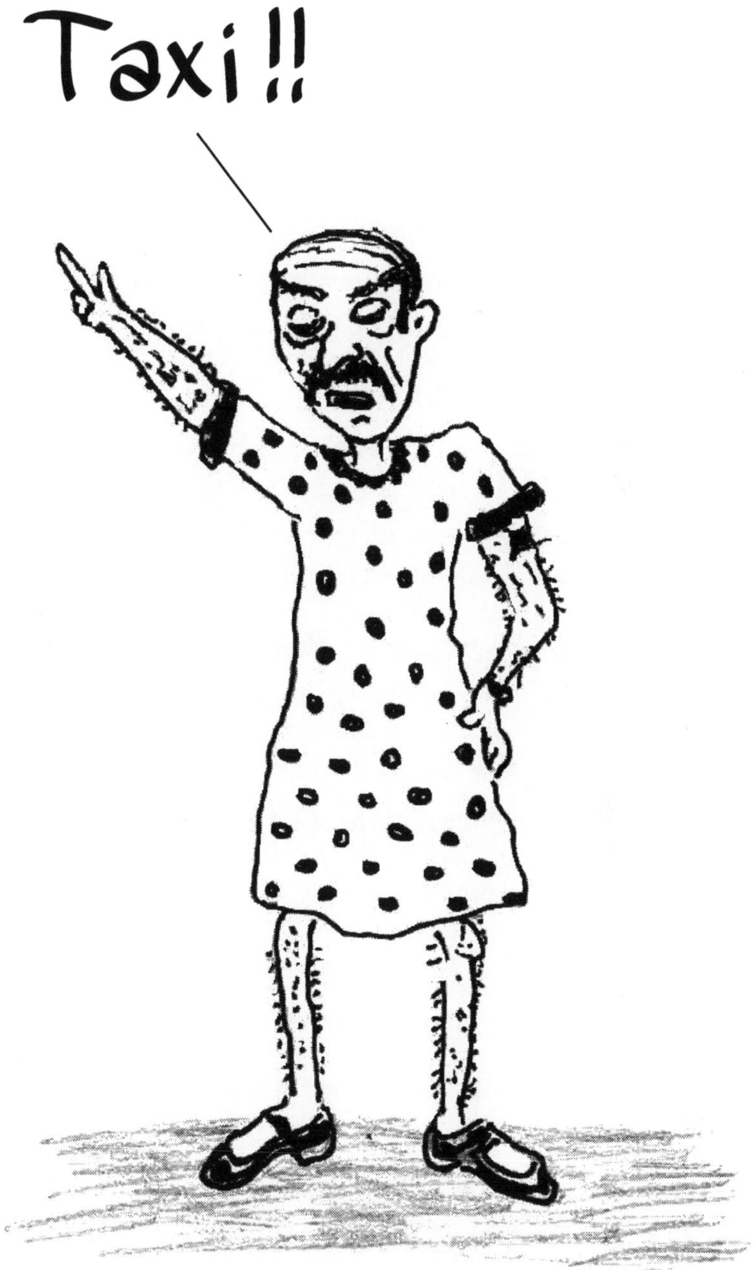
Taxi!!

EMERGENCY, MY TV REMOTE IS DEAD

We've heard much about the abuse of emergency services in recent years. Below is a selection of some of the more extreme cases where an ambulance actually attended a so-called 'emergency'.

'I'm an alcoholic and I've run out of booze, will you take me to the off licence?'

'I've got a blood blister on my little toe and it really hurts.'

'I called 999 because my bum needs wiping and I feel too tired to do it myself today.' (male, 35 years).

'Can someone come and turn the TV off, because the batteries in my remote are dead?'

'I've got a problem with my ears sticking out.'

'My wheelchair is stuck between the bed and the wall, could you move it please, as I don't want to bother the carers?'

All the above were genuine calls, although certainly not genuine emergencies.

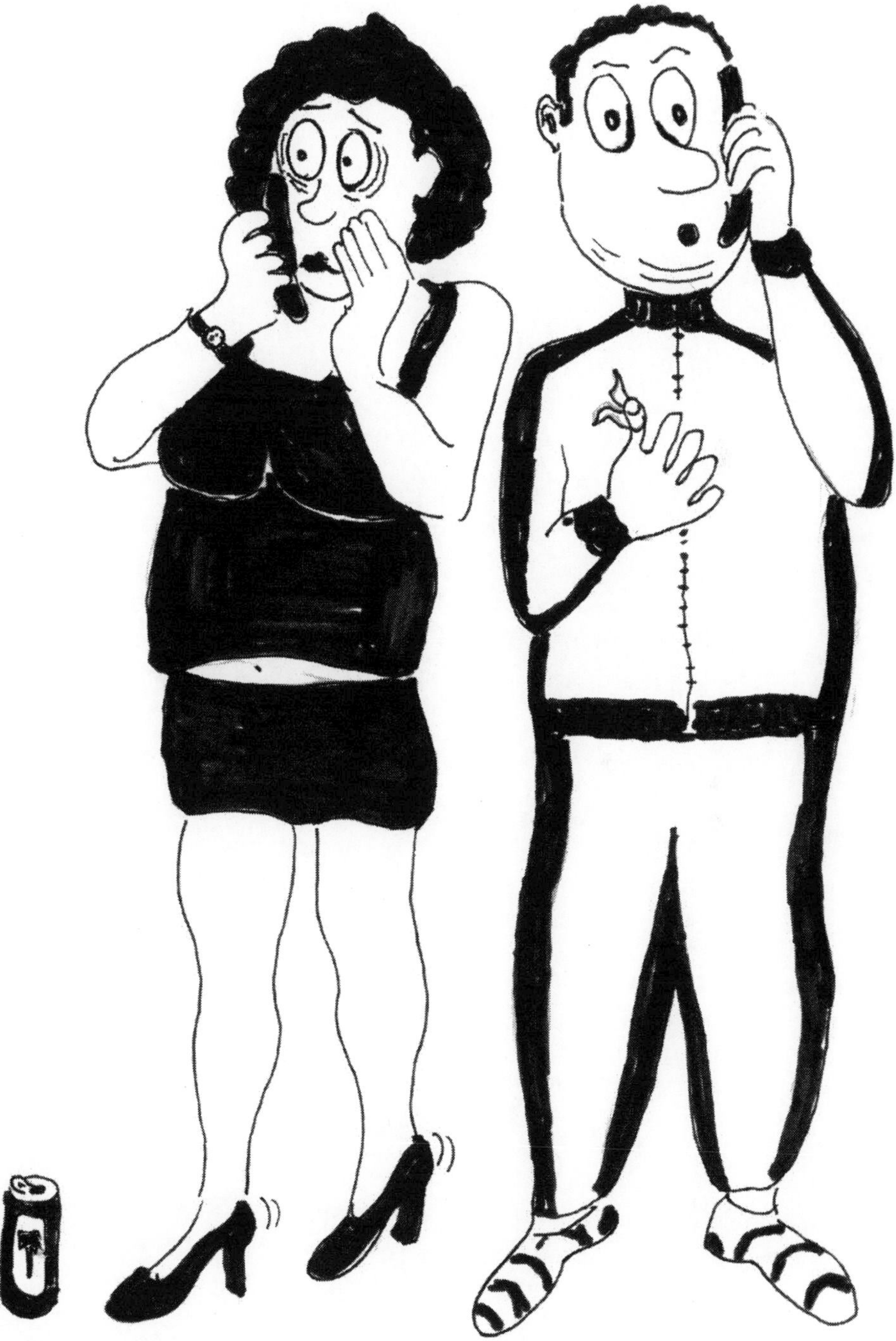

Printed in Great Britain
by Amazon.co.uk, Ltd.,
Marston Gate.